Skirts at War

SKIRTS AT WAR

Beyond Divorced Mom/Stepmom Conflict

Jennifer Newcomb Marine and Jenna Korf

CONTENTS

THE BIG PICTURE

In 2020, when the world was seemingly in lockdown free-fall, we revisited *Skirts at War* and decided that we'd learned so much since its original printing in 2013, it was time for an update. We've changed some exercises, arranged the format for easier navigation and added more relevant real-life examples.

We'll walk you through examples of common problems, exercises to fix them and journal questions to prompt deeper insights. You'll hear from readers, a remarried father's in-depth, private thoughts and from a divorced mom/stepmom who's thriving amidst a high-conflict situation.

We've taken the most important issues that moms and stepmoms struggle with and broken each subject down into three themes. You'll find those three keywords at the beginning of every chapter.

Here are the changes that are waiting for you

1. Your Strategic Advantage

- **Develop detachment skills:** learning to disconnect from traditional conflict is a life-changing superpower.
- **A context for pervasive stress:** understand why divorced-family issues feel so invasive and overwhelming.
- **Quick tools to use right now:** four effective techniques to calm your mind and body.

2. The Push and Pull of Power

- **Belonging drives behavior:** make your instinctual behavior visible and short-circuit reactions that cause even more problems.

- **The ownership of control:** understand the loss of the primal bond and your need to establish or repair it.
- **Independence without permission:** pick your battles with a unique filter (you may be surprised by what's easy to drop).

3. Simple Boundary Formulas

- **Commit to mastery:** learn what boundaries are and aren't, and pledge to overcome your fear and discomfort.
- **Enforce unpopular limits:** how-to steps for prioritizing problems and reshaping intractable conflicts without active cooperation from others.
- **Protect your soft spots:** manage the side effects of resistance to your new approach.

4. Increase Your Resilience

- **Recover from catastrophe:** expand your ability to withstand stress while maintaining equilibrium.
- **Relearn default responses:** renew your dedication to the basics of emotional management and self-care.
- **Practice makes imperfect:** integrate fun, nourishing daily practices into your habits and routines.

5. Choose Your Roles

- **Clarify your expectations:** discover the origins of our unspoken expectations and resentments-in-waiting.
- **Define real responsibilities:** sift through the tasks in need of change and identify areas of growth for others.
- **Set empowering limits:** learn how to delegate, withdraw participation and stop overdoing.

6. Helpful or Harmful Support

- **Become an advice detective:** discern the difference between encouraging and enabling agreement.
- **Deep comfort:** recognize the benefits of truthful feedback from friends and family.
- **Cultivate wisdom:** strengthen your support systems, get what you need and minimize drama.

7. Deciphering Men

- **For dads, from a dad:** learn from a remarried father's heartfelt, personal perspective.
- **The triangle of balance:** re-evaluate your ex's or husband's challenges as a partner and parent.
- **Recognize the contribution:** value his attempts to grow into his changing roles after divorce and remarriage.

8. Building Your Sanctuary

- **Create your refuge:** give yourself permission to escape to a delightful, self-made haven.
- **Prioritize renewal:** save space for the activities that bring you the most joy and soul-satisfaction.
- **Harness passionate dreams:** return to your goals outside of family life and realize your full potential.

9. One Reader's Story

- From *No One's the Bitch*, to *Skirts at War*, to eventual peace.

We hope you find the new edition helpful!

1

YOUR STRATEGIC ADVANTAGE

Detachment / Context / Quick Tools

Develop detachment skills

The ace up your sleeve

If you're a stepmom or divorced mom with a difficult, uncooperative counterpart, this book will help you cultivate the upper hand in problems between the houses—but not in the way you might think.

Your secret weapon?

The ability to detach and disengage. You'll learn how to win more divorce-connected family battles by not even participating in them at all.

We're going to help you become calmer, more unflappable and

self-possessed. You'll be less reactive, agitated and anxious. You'll
develop a higher perspective that will help you spot oncoming
problems a mile away, making it easier to sidestep them or
resolve them with aplomb.

We know what it's like to feel like the mom or stepmom is
making you miserable. Especially because her influence is so
pervasive, reaching into your home where you can't escape. You
may be feeling hopeless, overwhelmed and desperate for relief.

But unlike some other books in this field, we're not going to
spend a lot of time focusing on the other woman and how to
modify her behavior. Instead, we'll put the onus for change back
into your lap, because you have a lot more power, control and
freedom than you realize. We want to help you see it, reclaim it
and then use it wisely.

A context for pervasive stress

We need a bigger word

The problem between houses can be distilled down to a single
word: stress. But "stress" glosses over the painful reality of our
day-to-day experiences. Sometimes, it feels like everything you
do, no matter how well-intended, ends up being evaluated by
the other household and found lacking—especially things that
seemed just fine before by your own standards.

It's easy to think the other woman is the problem. If she'd just
go away, we'd feel so much better. That may be true, but what's
also true is that the bigger problem is the resulting tension we
end up with in these high-conflict situations. Learning how to
manage the stress of it all is what will benefit us the most.

Stepmoms: maybe she's sent you nasty texts or email messages,
or calls you the "other woman," even though you met years after
their split. Moms: perhaps she likes to "show" the kids how much
better she is than you at a variety of things or has let people

believe she's the mom by not correcting anyone who refers to her as such in public.

The good news: you're not crazy or emotionally inept if you're having a hard time, you aren't a failure for finding these issues so difficult, and you're not alone. See if you can relate to the most common triggers likely to set off divorced moms and stepmoms.

Situations in which you're likely to be triggered:

- Unwanted communication
- Money
- Breached privacy
- Hurtful, aggressive behavior
- Legal issues
- Financial decisions
- Control and power
- What's "best" for the kids
- Feeling excluded and helpless

If you nodded your head and checked off each item, don't despair! In the rest of this book, you're going to learn how to calm yourself during those intense, anxiety-ridden moments—or better yet—avoid them altogether.

In the words of our readers

> **Holly O.** (divorced mom, stepmom): "*My biggest trigger is what 'gets back to me' through family and mutual friends about how I am somehow failing the kids because of the differences in political and religious ideology between our households.*
>
> **Crystal B.** (stepmom): "*My husband's ex-wife would text him over twenty times a day. They were mainly complaints about him as a father or me as a stepmother. Even though he eventually learned to ignore them and turn his phone off, they were extremely intrusive.*

Wrangling the beast

It's vital for you to manage your stress well for a variety of reasons.

First, physically, the long-term effects of stress can be genuinely damaging. Second, because life is short! You don't want to spend it feeling constantly worried, anxious, and under assault. It's not enough to simply cope with all the demands that life presents to you. There's thriving and enjoying your life too. And third, managing and lowering stress will help you with all your relationships—not just with the other woman or the other household.

Now let's dive into how stress unfolds so that we learn what to do about it.

A jammed amygdala

Your amygdala is one of the oldest, most primitive parts of your brain. Think of it as a little almond-sized nugget left over when we were simpler beings, crawling through the mud. Over time, our brains developed to become the powerhouses that they are today.

The amygdala's job is to detect and defuse threats that might hurt you or kill you. It's the part of your brain that sees a wavy line in the grass and makes you jump before you've had time to think, "Snake!" Your amygdala is always at the ready, eager to protect you. But sometimes that wavy line in the grass is just a garden hose. Crisis averted! Then our nervous system calms down.

Usually, we can coast along, trusting our amygdala to do its thing in the background. Problems arise when it becomes hijacked by too much stress, becomes overactive and starts "seeing" snakes everywhere. Then your amygdala becomes not such a good friend. You're jumpy. Reacting without thinking. Tunnel vision makes you relentlessly focused on your problems.

We've seen this response frequently in these tech-connected times, where one person receives a barrage of abusive texts from the other.

Forget about seeing the bigger picture in this state. Your brainstorming abilities have gone out the window because your brain can't help but work to ensure your physical survival.

Two runners on a treadmill

Now that we know about that jumpy, little guard nugget above, the amygdala, let's add some background music. We have two key parts of our nervous system and they each have opposing jobs:

- **The Sympathetic**, or accelerator, helps us rev up, stay safe, and solve problems.
- **The Parasympathetic**, or the brakes, helps us relax and recover after the threat is gone.

When we perceive danger as we described above, our sympathetic nervous system kicks in and produces a stress response. Our bodies go into fight, flight, or freeze mode to respond to the threat. Our adrenal glands release hormones (adrenaline and cortisol), which causes an increased heart rate, muscle tension, and acute concentration as we Prepare for Battle!

After the danger has passed, we switch over to our parasympathetic nervous system for some good vibes. In the relaxation response, we're supposed to decompress and restore our equilibrium. Our bodies are self-healing while in this state, which is great. The problem is, faced with intense everyday stressors in our divorced and remarried families, many of us remain on "high alert" with our stress response continually activated. Not good for us.

Like it or not, we are tuned in to the radio station of our emotions. Even when you relive an upsetting event in your mind, your body doesn't treat it as just a memory. You may still react as if the event is happening right now again, negative hormones and all, prolonging the effects of stress on your body. Think back to the last time you were ill. You may have noticed that if you ruminated on a negative event, you felt much worse. But if you got some good news or even received a simple act of kindness, you felt better. It goes both ways.

When you're highly stressed both parts of your nervous system, the accelerator and the brakes, are struggling for dominance. Remember what it's like to be desperate for sleep, but have your mind racing as you replay the latest conflict with the other house? That's it in a nutshell. Feels awful.

Luckily, there are four quick and simple techniques you can use on the fly to create some immediate relief. Later on in the book, we'll provide you with additional emotional reset tools for when you have more time, focus and privacy.

Let's get started.

Quick tools to use right now

The window of tolerance

When you're in the middle of that fight-flight-freeze response (or being triggered) it can feel like quite a challenge to pull yourself out of it. The key is to widen your window of tolerance, which means expanding your ability to manage the ups and downs of emotions without going into the stress response.

> The "Window of Tolerance" (Ogden, et al. (2006); Siegel, 1999) is the optimal zone of arousal where we are able to manage and thrive in everyday life. This can be thought of as sailing within a river of well-being (Siegel & Bryson, 2012) where we are able to respond to all that comes our way without getting thrown off course.

When we're outside our window of tolerance and our nervous system responds with fight-flight-freeze, we'll either feel spaced out, numb and shut down (hypoarousal), or we'll feel panicky and overwhelmed (hyperarousal). Our goal is to remain in that window of tolerance as often as possible.

We can do this by deliberately helping our brain recalibrate how it detects danger. By intentionally changing our physical state, our vagus nerve (part of our parasympathetic nervous system) sends signals to our brain that we are not in a life-threatening situation when the other woman insults us by text message or our stepchild shuns us.

Wouldn't it be great to stay calmer and more centered with the things that throw you for a loop?

Try one of these four recalibrating techniques the next time you're upset:

- Notice your emotions and body.
- Exhale long and change your posture.
- Move to expel adrenaline.
- Name what you're experiencing.

Notice your emotions and body

If you can pay closer attention to how you're feeling physically and emotionally, a couple of new things will happen.

One, you'll become much more aware of your predictable reactions to common triggers. That awareness will help you transition from a hijacked amygdala to staying in the present. Two, you'll be able to quickly sense the very beginnings of tension and interrupt the fall into stronger negative emotions. The more you practice this, the easier and more automatic it becomes.

Exhale long and change your posture

Exhaling engages your parasympathetic nervous system and calms you down. Gently breathe out longer than you're breathing in. Paying attention to that sensation immediately changes your physiology. Now you can come more easily back into a state where your logical brain is back online and make conscious choices.

While you're doing some soft, deep exhales, adjust your posture so that you're sitting up straighter and more centered. Lengthen your neck and your spine. Remember that feeling of strength and pride that you have when you're feeling good. Shifting your body like this can create those positive emotions, even if it's just in smaller doses.

Move to expel adrenaline

When you start to feel antsy or anxious, it's time to release the surge of adrenaline that's pumping through your veins. That rush of energy is meant to help us fight or run—so get to it, but safely!

Start by finding somewhere you can be alone and get physical. Think of how a child has a tantrum: kids are great at expelling that energy. Some suggestions for movement include pumping your arms in the air like you're protesting to the gods, doing jumping jacks, dancing with intensity, speed walking, jogging around your neighborhood, or working out at a gym. You could also try punching a pillow, mattress, or punching bag, or screaming in your car or bedroom (if no one is home). Even shaking your body as if there were June bugs on your skin and you were trying to get them off works!

Then after you feel better, you might want to cry or make some sighing and groaning noises. Whatever wants to come out of you, let it. Then be kind to yourself and give yourself some comforting compassion.

Name what you're experiencing

Lastly, naming what you feel can be very effective. When we bring something out of the shadows and into the light by acknowledging it, it holds less power over us. Categorizing a challenging experience also engages our prefrontal cortex, the part of our brain that's involved in higher-level, more analytical thinking, such as problem-solving. Feelings and sensations can flow, then be released.

Ask yourself:

What is happening right now? What's bothering me about it? What emotions am I feeling? How does my body feel?

Go somewhere you can be alone, and either mouth, whisper, or say out loud whatever comes to your mind about what's going on. Be honest about it too, not polite. You're not performing for anyone and no one will ever know what you're saying or feeling. You're allowed the full range of these very human emotions and responses. They don't make you a bad person.

For example, you might say, "Ugh, I'm feeling so threatened right now. I hate when my partner has to talk to her. I feel so small. Ignored. Powerless. *I hate her!* I wish she was gone. My shoulders are tense and my stomach feels tight. My neck hurts. I just effing hate this situation and wish I never had to see her *ever again!*"

After you give voice to your thoughts and feelings, see if it's easier to take a step back. Hopefully, after saying what you had to say, you feel validated and calmer.

This tool can take some practice if you're not used to voicing such negativity, or if you're judging yourself. But keep practicing it and give yourself the chance to experience the benefits.

Like storm clouds blowing through

You might have noticed that none of these tools above are about denying your feelings or suppressing your physical experience. Instead, they're about embracing them, working with them and befriending even the most uncomfortable sensations.

Over time, as we experiment with these tools, they can help to retrain our nervous system. We will grow in confidence as we learn to trust ourselves to handle even the most nerve-racking situations. We will have widened our window of tolerance and expanded our ability to weather the strong winds of any storm, however imperfectly.

In the words of our readers

K.K. (divorced mom, stepmom): *"After months of court proceedings, an order was made, and the mom decided she would not follow it. I was so angry I made myself ill with stress. It would have been helpful if people around me had said more forcefully, 'Hey, this is so not you,' earlier on when I started getting so angry a few months ago. I'm coming to a better place with it all now, and catch myself when I am about to start a tirade about the mom."*

Alissa (divorced mom): *"The worst feeling in the world was getting my reputation pulled through the mud and my parenting put under a microscope in order to win a court battle."*

Jenna's story

I won't presume to know what belief my husband's ex must have had about me that would cause her to treat me the way she did. But mostly her communications to me and my husband were so bad that eventually the sound of a text message on either of our phones would make my heart jump out of my chest and my stomach knot. My heart raced when I checked my email for fear of what I'd be accused of this time.

I now know I was experiencing PTSD (Post Traumatic Stress Disorder) symptoms from her communications. And since the original writing of this book, I've worked with hundreds of stepmoms who have also experienced PTSD from the way they're being treated by the ex. Aggression and constant verbal and emotional attacks are abusive behaviors, and they can be traumatic.

It took implementing three different strategies for me to stop having that automatic response to the text message sounds.

The first is we finally got to the point in our situation where we could both block her texts. That gave me the knowledge that the text coming through couldn't be from her. I was safe. The second was that I replaced the text tone with a different, more soothing tone. That helped retrain my brain and nervous system by breaking the association between the sound and the message.

And the third thing I did was use the original text tone that triggered me for something positive. I used it as my Paypal notification that I received funds from my work. So now when I received a text it was a tone that was new and soothing to me, and when I heard the old triggering tone, it meant something good had happened. It took a while to heal from that PTSD, but what I learned was that a crucial step in healing is to protect yourself from what's causing it.

Jennifer's story

Well! A lot has changed in my life since writing this book. While working on the first edition, I met and married my husband. One would think after writing about divorced families for so long, I would have been a model stepmom to my three (then) teen stepchildren. But no. I made every mistake in the book—and then some, just to be fancy.

I was lucky enough to "inherit" a friendly, cooperative ex-wife in my situation and for that, I'll be forever grateful. My husband rarely complained about her and she seemed happy enough to deal with just him for kid-related matters. She even read my first book, which felt a little too close to home in some ways, though I appreciated her efforts to create a working bridge between us.

My problems came from feeling caught in the middle… Between my partner and his kids. My own kids and my partner. The two sets of children. My relationship and the kids, period. It was messy, confusing and truth be told, pretty overwhelming.

I can't tell you how many times I found myself distraught and upset, torn between conflicting loyalties and wondering how in the world I was ever going to untangle all these interlocking puzzles.

In ways both subtle and overt, I butted heads with each of my wonderful stepchildren. I agonized over feeling like I was neglecting my own children, pouring so much energy and time into being a good stepmom by helping my husband.

Like I said, total rookie stuff.

Enter the power of excellent therapy. Through it, I learned about the consequences of not having healthy personal boundaries, better communication and saving some of my vital life force for me and me alone.

We're empty nesters now (and have a granddaughter!). Life seems a lot simpler in our still divorce-connected family household, but there are still those occasional echoes of earlier challenges. I have learned so much in the process and wish I would have known then what I know now. We hope our mistakes will save you from making some of your own.....

Mantras for managing stress

- "The goal isn't to always be at peace, it's to excel at managing life's stressors."
- "With practice, I can learn to become less triggered."
- "When my nervous system is activated, I can pause and restore my feeling of safety."
- "I have compassion for the stress and trauma I've endured."
- "I am committed to tending to my nervous system and learning how to regulate it."

2

THE PUSH AND
PULL OF POWER

Belonging / Control / Independence

Belonging drives behavior

Losing your team

The first place to start when talking about conflicts over power is one of the most sensitive, tender areas of life as human beings: belonging. Besides the basics, like air, water, food, and shelter; belonging is one of our core needs. It's that instant feeling of acceptance and support that is conferred by family—either the one you grew up in, or the one you make as an adult.

With your family, you're part of an imperfect, but complete team. You go through the good times together and the bad. Everyone's included, quirky annoyances and all. You make shared memories, and establish a foundation of essential building blocks and developmental milestones, such as marriage, birth, school, work and death.

Deep in your heart, belonging feels like being part of a whole that is its own little universe—like it's you and your little family against the hardships of the world.

But here is where it can get tricky… because when a family goes through a divorce, that universe is altered forever. A divorce represents the end for parents and kids. But for a new stepmom or remarried mom, her new world is just beginning. Each side has a changed perspective now. There are different feelings, expectations, hopes, and dreams….

How belonging gets broken

Let's back up a bit. The last thing a mother imagines when she's pregnant (such excitement and anticipation!) is that she may someday have to share her babies (or their father) with another woman—even if she and her husband can't stand each other by the time they divorce. Children are expecting to take their cues from the same, lifelong, primary caregivers. Parents are "supposed" to stay together to raise their dependent young until they're ready to leave the nest eighteen years later.

And when a woman falls in love and gets married, the last thing she's thinking is that she'll be okay having her partner remain forever connected to another woman.

Now, each parent is left putting back the pieces alone or, eventually, with a new partner. That sense of safety and support, of automatic belonging, is thrown into upheaval. Each adult involved in a divorce or remarriage must try to create a new intact universe, with new milestones and memories. That takes time to build. And in the meantime, there are plenty of opportunities to feel awkward, hurt, out of place, and downright ostracized.

For both women, the presence of the other often feels weird

and wrong. Yet, somehow, we're supposed to just know how to manage a situation that goes against the very fiber of our beings and do it with good manners, flexibility, and smiles on our faces. Fat chance.

Here are some of the unique ways divorced moms and stepmoms experience a sense of disrupted belonging:

Divorced moms

- An ongoing sense of grief and heartbreak over the broken container for your once-intact family, even if you'd rather not be married to your ex anymore. Whether you were left or the one who did the leaving, you try to keep this one buried deep.
- Sadness and disappointment that it's so hard to create a new family with someone who's not the biological parent of your children (and wouldn't die trying to save their lives), whether as a newly single mom or a remarried mom.
- The fear that your children now have an unresolvable strike against them in life because they came from a broken family and won't do as well as other children who have the stability of two married parents in a nuclear family.
- The rituals of the past that brought so much joy are tinged with the absence of the other parent or perhaps even ruined altogether. You don't know what to replace them with.

Stepmoms

- The weight of the past can feel so much stronger than your relationship will ever be—all those memories and formative experiences you weren't a part of (pregnancy, birth, toddlerhood, etc.)—but the kids, your partner, and all the relatives were. It can seem like you'll never "catch up" in terms of importance, bond, or significance.

- A feeling like you're always going to be second best, an outsider, an intruder. Having imposter syndrome, like you shouldn't have a full say in decisions and preferences. You might yearn to have children just so you can also feel cemented into the family structure.
- It's like you're always living with the echo of the previous relationship reverberating throughout your house. Just ask any stepmom who has cleaned out the garage and found a boxful of old photos from her partner's first wedding.
- You often give more value or weight to the "firsts" your partner had with the ex, so there's insecurity around "firsts" that are yours—marriage, baby, buying a house, etc. You're afraid your partner won't be as excited, or have a feeling of "already been there, done that," even though most of the time it's a completely different experience for your partner.

Creating a new family universe

So how can you reduce the sting of all those experiences listed above? For starters, think of your life as a novel that has jumped forward in time. You're starting a fresh chapter, with new people and circumstances.

One thing for stepmoms to keep in mind is that it often takes four to seven years for a stepfamily to go through specific stages of stepfamily development that culminate in feeling—and functioning—like a family. For divorced moms, if you're newly split, you will all need time to heal and create a new family unit that still feels whole, healthy, and complete.

So remember: you're playing the long game.

See if you can cultivate patience, allow relationships to evolve, and make a conscious effort to create opportunities for small connections and new family rituals, memories, and traditions. This can come in the form of meals, weekend activities, or bedtime routines. It can be as simple as having a movie or game night, or eating dessert first every Friday night.

It will help to have the kids' buy-in here, so as a starting point, ask them what they like, think about what will be fun for them and take that into consideration. You might need to try many different things before you discover what works for your family. Some traditions may even appear by accident and sometimes those are the best ones!

For stepmoms in particular, we recommend going into this with the mindset of trial and error as opposed to thinking you must come up with the perfect way to bond with your family. With divorced moms or remarried moms, keep the bigger picture in mind: you're modeling flexibility, stability, and moving forward into a new life.

For both women, try to relax into the process and be curious about what's possible.

The ownership of control

Wrestling for dominance

It's one of the worst feelings in the world: you're doing your absolute best to fix an unpleasant situation, but still can't make it any better, no matter how hard you try. The kinds of problems we're describing in this book are draining, demoralizing, and seem never-ending too. We're forced out of conversations that directly affect us or the children. We are told by someone else what we can or cannot do.

Over time, after a series of defeats and intractable struggles that go nowhere, you may feel acutely overwhelmed. Worst of all, the other side cannot be bested, because they're trying just as hard as you are and seem to have limitless endurance.

Sometimes we don't realize that what we're feeling is utter powerlessness, because it's covered up by our anger about the situation. If you're banging your head against the wall again and again, there could be a powerful, but hidden cause.

The battle of emotional bonds

One reason dual-household families can seem so impossible is because we have the two most important relationships of our lives competing against each other: parent and child versus romantic relationship. This creates a dynamic in relationships that we like to call "emotional authority."

Family members often feel like the strength of their bonds to other family members automatically confers upon them certain rights, certain "givens." The intensity and purity of your love for another seems to equal more power, more say in what happens to them. It's as if that person is "yours," even though on the surface that sounds ridiculous. We're already familiar with how this works in traditional relationships, especially in nuclear families.

Think about it. When you were growing up, your mother (or primary caretaker) was typically the one directing your life: making decisions about your diet, daily activities, sleep schedule, playdates, health-related issues, schooling, etc.

Just as in nature, we take for granted that our mother or caretaker would protect us against any perceived threats, such as bullies in school or extended family members who might not have our best interests at heart—all in an effort to nurture and love us, without giving her actions a second thought. Some of us didn't grow up in nurturing households and suffered at the hands of neglectful or abusive parents, but nevertheless, we know the archetype well.

As a society, we also have certain "givens" for a romantic

relationship. Spouses and cohabitating romantic partners confide in each other about the most intimate matters. Traditionally, they make financial decisions together, attend to household chores, and do their best to form a consensus on parenting values. They're loyal to each other and monogamous. They protect their right to dictate what happens in their household. They relax together, pick up the slack for each other, and rest in the safety of knowing their partner has their back.

But what if you have two households that use emotional authority to make decisions that aren't aligned with the other household? Let's cross the loyalty lines a bit and see what happens.

Our superior agenda

When we act from a sense of emotional authority, our powerful feelings make it easy to discount the other person's concerns in favor of our own. Our agenda is superior since it's based on love and fierce attachment. (And yes, fear as well, if we're feeling threatened, which makes both parties try even harder to exert control, even if we end up making things worse.)

We couldn't let go of our emotional authority even if we tried, nor would we want to.

This dynamic sets us up for clashes of the worst kind, since it is rooted in either maternal instincts of protection—or romantic attachments to the person we have chosen as our mate. Figuring out how to "work with" the other side is confusing and emotionally charged because taking a step back feels like betraying our loved ones and abdicating our responsibilities to them. This response applies equally to moms and stepmoms, even if the outward details are different.

Let's say the stepmom is largely responsible for overseeing her stepchild's homework in her home as dad works full time and is less available. She knows her stepson has been struggling in school after witnessing many nights of homework that ended in tears. For the past two years, mom, dad, and stepmom have all had access to the child's teachers and school records. But now that he's doing worse in school, out of nowhere, mom revokes stepmom's privileges and lets the school know that she no longer wants the stepmom involved. The stepmom is thinking, "What the hell? I've already been at this for two years now. I care about helping my stepson. My partner wants me to help, so that's reason enough to be involved." Meanwhile, the mom is thinking "It's my ex's job to stay on top of this, not the stepmom's. Who does she think she is? Why do we need one more person complicating everything? She needs to just let the parents handle this and take a step back!"

Believe it or not, the stepmom might feel some of the same mother tiger instincts that a mother would feel, especially if she's known the kids since they were very young. (Along with some indignation at being controlled by the other person.) What happens when the mom tries to pull rank with a stepmom who feels connected and concerned about her stepson after all these years, just as she would with her own son? A power struggle!

As for the mom, she remembers when it was just herself and her ex handling school matters. They had separate parent-teacher conferences so they wouldn't have to be in the same room. Now there's another woman who feels like she "has the right" to be included in communications with her child's teacher. Mom tried to go with the flow and be respectful, but she's had enough. She's supposed to be inclusive and endlessly flexible? Says who? It can certainly seem as if one side is always the winner or the loser in our divorce-connected families. A huge priority for you regarding your child, stepchild, or romantic partner can be a confounding and absolute "No" for the other party—and they will not budge.

In the example above, both stepmom and mom were likely experiencing a strong sense of emotional jurisdiction because their actions came from love and concern for the child.

The onset of the Covid-19 pandemic in 2020 highlighted one common area for dual-household power struggles: *medical issues.*

At the time of this update, many stepfamilies and single-parent families are being forced to deal with behaviors from the other household that not only *feel* life-threatening, but potentially are. One parent or stepparent might have a very laissez-faire attitude about the pandemic as they ignore recommended health guidelines by government officials. If friends were behaving this way, the more cautious stepmom or divorced mom could say, "I'll see you when I feel it's safe for me to do so." But in these family situations, she can't do that. She's forced to interact with family members who have been put at risk and now increase the risk for others as well.

Again, compromising when it comes to protecting the health and safety of loved ones will feel like you're betraying them. This is a high-stakes disagreement that is difficult to resolve.

In the words of our readers

> **Lauren T. (stepmom)**: *"When there is lack of respect, everything else crumbles. There is name-calling, verbal attacks, and tons of judgment. It creates two sides, rather than a team for the children. When there is respect, mistakes (which everyone makes!) can become learning experiences, rather than opportunities to blame and point fingers."*

> **K.F. (mom, stepmom)**: *"We have sub-families in our house: my husband and stepson, and my son and me. After 11 years together, that line still hasn't blended."*

Emotional authority assumptions

Now that you have a better understanding of emotional authority and how it can often place you in a power struggle with the other person, let's look at your emotional rights, and see how they might connect to power struggles with the other woman or household. Examples would include:

- "I care for my stepson most of the time, therefore I have a right to be at the parent-teacher conferences."
- "Conferences are for parents only, since we know our children the best."
- "Only I'm allowed to take my daughter for haircuts. That's a mom thing."
- "If I see that no one is tending to my stepchild's hair, I'm going to step up and do the right thing."
- "I have to live with the kids too and have a right to control behavior that happens in my home."
- "I have a right to speak with my ex about the kids without his partner present."
- "This is my house and I shouldn't have to hear my stepson's mom's voice on Facetime every day."
- "Just because my children are at their father's house, it doesn't mean my relationship ends with them during their time there."

Journal questions: Emotional authority assumptions

Name three concise emotional rights you assume are "yours," based on a sense of emotional authority, whether the other household agrees with you or not.

- It's helpful to brainstorm what the other person's givens are too based on their behaviors. Remember, even if you disagree, knowing what they consider to be their rights based on emotional authority may provide you with deeper insights into what is driving their behavior in a specific situation.

- Once you have your list, share it with your partner or a close friend.

- If you're a stepmom, ask your partner what they think about it. Discuss where these particular beliefs might have come from. How do they manifest themselves in your relationship and family? Are there consequences to these beliefs? Consider how these beliefs might conflict with your female counterpart and how that plays out.

· You may decide that there's something you've been doing that you want to change. Or not.

· At the very least, you may decipher a confusing or frustrating behavior of hers and create some protective distance between the two of you.

Extra Credit: What do you think some of her rights are, even if you disagree with them?

Financial pain points

Clashing emotional bonds between households are challenging enough. Add finances to the mix and things can spiral out of control. Money is essential to our survival, but it's also a volatile, unpredictable resource. There are entire books on money and divorced/blended families, so for now, we'll just touch on the subject.

See if you can relate to some of the biggest complaints stepmoms and divorced moms have about money. Place a check mark next to your biggest concerns.

Stepmoms

- Staying home to take care of the kids and feeling financially dependent.
- How financial dependence affects your relationship, financial decisions, sense of confidence, etc…
- Whether to have a separate or combined bank account.
- The ex excludes the stepmom from her child's life, but includes her income in child support.
- The partner who pays above and beyond his required child support.
- Feeling like her side goes "without" because of his

generosity with the ex.

- Her "ours" child suffers because so much money goes to the ex and the other children.
- We can't have an "ours" child because of financial instability due to court, ongoing conflict, etc…
- Clashing with her husband, who wants to give his children everything.

Divorced moms

- Having just one income as a single mom, compared to the two of a remarried dad.
- A single mom who can't afford to go to court.
- A father allocating more money to his own kids with the stepmom.
- Feeling like the stepmom is behind the father's new financial decisions with his kids.
- A remarried mom whose husband prioritizes his own children financially over her children.
- A father prioritizes his wife's preferences about extras for the kids.
- Saving for college from child support when you can barely pay your bills.
- Feeling like your children have been "forgotten" in favor of your ex's new children.
- Being compared to a stay-at-home stepmom, and all she does for the kids when you have to work.

Reduce the number of battles

Would you like to minimize the number of power struggles between the households?

To start, let's take inventory by reviewing the diagram below. Which groups of people have been a challenge for you? Which life areas? Imagine the number of overlapping lines between family members in our dual-family (or tri-family) situations, like a service map in an airline magazine. Don't forget about extended family, step in-laws—and because of the high rate of divorce for stepfamilies—former stepmoms, stepdads and stepchildren.

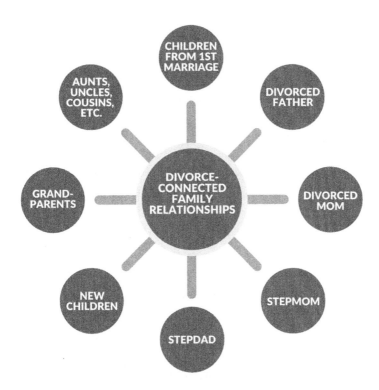

Let's face it, there are a lot of characters involved in this drama and plenty of life areas that are affected. One important option open to you is to reduce the number of hills you're willing to die on. Let a few things go that you might normally insist on changing and turn your attention to the areas of life where you've already proven you can make a positive difference.

If you consider the complexity of all these relationships, and all these life areas, it is no wonder that we're often encountering conflict. A hard truth: there's no absolute fairness in stepfamilies and divorce-connected households. You will lose battles you don't think you should lose. This is a challenging path for even the hardiest soul. So while you may balk at the idea of letting the other side "get away" with any more than they already have, engaging less is a powerful way to bring back some additional peace to your life.

Track your values, not your wins

One way to take part in fewer battles is to focus on the values that you choose to emphasize in the long run in your family.

A value is an internal judgment about what is important to an individual. There are no morally right or wrong values. A single value can mean different things to different people. Values are intangible; they are not something you do or have. Meditation is not a value, but it is an activity that may help one honor the value of spirituality. Some examples of values are:

- Inclusion
- Acceptance
- Intimacy
- Predictability
- Connection
- Honesty
- Hard work

Divorce-connected families are rife with differences in values. For example, one parent may often let the child stay home from school, driving the other parent nuts. One parent rates "education" and "responsibility" as two of their highest values, while the parent who frequently lets the child stay home from school values "freedom" and "independence." When another person disregards one of your most important values, it can feel extremely invalidating. Can you see how these different priorities set up the two households for years of disagreements and confrontations?

When you're engaged in a power struggle, you can lose sight of the intentions behind your actions. Are you protecting and honoring what's important to you, or are you exerting power because someone told you that you can't? Take, for example, the stepmom who goes to every Little League game. She spends three hours every weekend because she wants to show the ex she isn't going anywhere and has a right to be there. But is the stepmom really winning here? That's a lot of wasted time and the result is often built-up resentment and a lost sense of self. She might have started out valuing loyalty, commitment, or support, but then devolved into something less helpful (and more personally stressful!).

To create some extra space in a difficult situation, think about all the areas you feel in conflict with the other woman, and your actions in response. Can you pinpoint the difference between a genuine conflict in values and a power struggle?

Journal questions: What's important to me?

What are your top five most important values?

1. _____

2. _____

3. _____

4. _____

5. _____

Think about some common areas of conflict with the other household. What is actually a clashing of values between households?

Independence without permission

A stranger in the house

One thing that's hard to get people to understand if they're not in a dual-household (or more!) situation themselves is how incredibly difficult it is to have the other woman, the other family, present in your daily life. Normally, as you go through life, you're doing your best to face the unknown, make mistakes, fix them and fumble your way forward. It's hard enough all on its own. But when you throw another person into the mix who's now opposing you, everything can feel ten times harder.

When a romantic couple without children splits up, that's generally it. You go your separate ways with separate lives, separate homes, and often separate sets of friends and family. You're done. And you're glad!

Not in these set-ups, as you already know all too well.

Now the other woman in your life is like an infiltrator, an invader, trumping decisions and milestones that should be yours. For divorced moms, she may be involved at school, plastering photos of herself and the kids on social media, or helping your daughter plan her wedding. None of these scenarios are necessarily wrong, but they don't fit with the vision you had for yourself as a mom.

For stepmoms, she may keep your partner in a never-ending custody battle, making it financially harder for you to have your own child together, or she may prevent you from participating in important medical conversations regarding your ill stepchild. Her attempt to control things regarding her children has a direct impact on aspects of your life that no one except you should get to control.

The other woman may impact even minor things. She's there in the way you have to schedule your days, your weeks, and your year. You see her in the children's behavior, maybe even in their facial features. She's there in your ex's new stance on a subject that used to not be a problem. It feels like nothing is yours anymore.

Focus on the freedom you already have

There's a concept called learned helplessness in psychology. Basically, if a person is repeatedly subjected to a negative stimulus that they cannot escape (especially in childhood), they may just stop trying anything in response, even when they can make the situation better.

So how can you decrease the drama if you can't get away from it? One of the best ways to combat helplessness is to focus on the areas of freedom and control you already have in your life. Many of us overlook the opportunity to do this, because we're so busy focusing on the things outside of our control and trying to fix them.

Sometimes, if we pay attention to that intuitive voice telling us to prioritize what makes us happy, we face some formidable inner obstacles. We get in our own way with guilt and fear of confrontation or standing up for ourselves. We're afraid of expressing our preferences, of being rude and selfish.

But it's okay to honor what you want and see it as valid. It's okay to fulfill your own needs, even if you don't know what you're doing. You can even go about it clumsily, without grace or tact. It's also okay if your partner gets upset with you about it sometimes. You deserve to hold some of your life energy back just for you.

So what areas of our lives do we all have control over? Here are some that might not be so obvious:

- How we spend our time.
- How we spend our money.
- Who we choose to be around (if you think this isn't true, just ask a stepmom who remained married but moved into her own little one-bedroom apartment

because her stepchildren were intolerable).
- How much time and energy we spend thinking about a particular person or topic.
- What behavior from other people we will tolerate (much more about this in the chapter on boundaries).

Hopefully you're starting to see that you might have more power over your life than you thought. We want to be clear that we're not saying that the actions required to control those areas of our lives are easy or simple to take. We acknowledge that they may upset the status quo and may even cause temporary conflict in your relationships, but that doesn't mean they're not worth taking.

Give up on changing her

We've found that one of the biggest regrets women in high-conflict situations have is how many years they wasted wishing the other woman would change—or even trying to make her. They spent so much energy focused on her behavior that they unintentionally neglected their own children, their well-being, and every other aspect of their life. We don't want you to have those same regrets.

But despite your best efforts, you may still slip into the following thoughts:

- "Maybe if I'm nicer to her…"
- "Maybe if I appease her…"
- "Maybe if I ignore her…"
- "Maybe if I kill her with kindness…"
- "Maybe if I just model how a real grown-up would do it, then she will ____."

These are all still attempts to change her behavior. People in high-conflict cannot see your good intentions or hear words meant to help. Sometimes we can give others a new perspective that might lead to insight on their behalf, but this usually only happens with people with which we already have an established relationship. Not quite the description of your relationship with the mom or stepmom in your life, right?

Regardless of the boundaries you set with the other party, there will be times when they will just flagrantly do what they want. Whatever is going on with her, whatever is fueling her unwanted behavior, realize that the cause is bigger than you. Release yourself from this burden of trying to make her change. Lighten your load. Honor your own moral standards as best you can and repeat to yourself, "I am not responsible for her actions. I release the need to control her."

We know it's lousy to feel like you're the only one sucking it up and shouldering all the weight, but if you want to create positive change, you must accept responsibility. That means, right now, right here in this moment while you're reading this book, you must say to yourself (silently or out loud):

- "I'm going to stop trying to change and control her."
- "I'm going to focus instead on where I can actually make a difference—and that's with myself."
- "From this point on, I will stop the behavior that is not getting me anywhere."

Helpful mind games

You may slip back into a power struggle with the other woman and not even know it until you're upset. To turn the focus back onto the power you already have and the decisions you can still make without interference, there's a little mind game you can play.

Ask yourself: if the other woman was to suddenly apologize to you and treat you with respect, what would you do differently? Make a list of those things. Especially note all the things that affect your time, energy, mood and physical space.

If an imagined apology is too much of a stretch, then try a little science fiction magic.

Journal questions: The time machine

If you traveled to the future in a time machine and could see that the other side/household would never act any differently...

- What would you do to save your sanity and reduce the drama?

- What would you stop doing? What would you start doing?

- If the other woman wasn't there, what would you be focusing on? What parts of your life have you been neglecting since this situation started?

- If she was going to take up a lot less space in your life, what would that look like?

The goal is to focus more on your own quality of life because that is in your control.

There will still be times when a part of you will still want to hold her responsible and force her to do things differently so you can be more comfortable. When you can, catch yourself in the act, course correct, and prevent the downward mental spiral that usually follows.

Focus on what is your responsibility, the dynamic in your household, and make changes as you see fit.

In the words of our readers

> **Meg (stepmom)**: *"It's unnatural to have a woman who openly hates me be so involved in every aspect of my life. It's unnatural to not be able to be myself, open, loving, goofy, etc., out of fear of stealing the mom's thunder. It's unnatural that I don't get to make decisions with my husband. I have to include his ex in a lot of daily decisions."*

M.E. (stepmom): *"Her telling the kids that she can't buy them _____ (fill in the blank) because daddy doesn't pay enough; the allegations of abuse and neglect submitted to court; hearing from my stepkids that 'Mom doesn't like you,' it all infuriates me."*

Jenna's story

As I reflect back, I'm realizing that if my husband's ex wouldn't have tried to exclude me at every turn and disrespect my marriage, I would have been able to do something differently. For instance, I wouldn't have needed to show up at every lacrosse game I really didn't want to be at. I'm realizing some of the things I did were solely in response to feeling like she was trying to control me, to invalidate me as a person and my place in the kids' and my husband's life, so in response I was saying HERE I AM.

If I imagine that she had just said to me, "Hey, we're a team now. I'm glad the kids like you", there would have been nothing for me to feel I had to protect. There would have been no power struggle to engage in. But the problem with placing the blame on her is that it puts all the power to change things in her hands. Instead, I took the actions that were in my control. I created some strong boundaries around our communication. I stopped giving her access to me, and I protected myself from the unwanted behavior.

Jennifer's story

As I mentioned in the last chapter, my relationships with my kids' stepmom and my husband's ex-wife have, luckily, been relatively trouble-free. Most my stress came from the disconnect between the world I used to inhabit as a mother of two… and a new stepmom to three teens. That normal feeling of being in control, making decisions, following up with consequences that felt fitting and appropriate—all those things flew out the window.

I encountered both a warm welcome and steep resistance from my stepkids, which in some ways made their behavior even more confusing. I felt like an athlete that had transferred to a different sport. Now I was clumsy, inept, had no strength or endurance and, what's more, people didn't like me!

What made it all so much worse is that my husband and I couldn't see eye-to-eye on even defining the problems between me and his kids. I had no idea that I was bumping up against loyalty binds between him and his children and kept expecting him to have my back more, only to feel sorely disappointed and hurt.

It took us working through our own complicated issues for me to feel more settled in this role. I had to let go of so many things and loosen my grip. I had to take a step back and release the vision of some gloriously integrated stepfamily and just allow things to land where they would. Of course, it's also easier, now that everyone has long since flown the coop. I discovered that, sometimes, the more you try to have power, the less you have, because you're trying to find it in places where it doesn't exist.

Mantras for reclaiming power

- "I honor my needs for belonging and emotional authority."
- "Not everyone will like me and I will not like everyone."
- "It's okay to not have a relationship with my partner's ex."
- "I focus on what is within my control."
- "I will spend my energy on my highest values."

3

SIMPLE BOUNDARY FORMULAS

Commit / Enforce / Protect

Commit to mastery

Protecting yourself from unwanted behavior

The word "boundaries" gets thrown around a lot these days. But they're one of the most misunderstood concepts in interpersonal relationships and most people don't know how to use them to their full potential.

A boundary is simply a limit you set with someone without any kind of assured response or reaction. It's a way of communicating to someone who has crossed a line. "If you continue this unwanted behavior, then this is how I will respond."

Since we can't control others, a boundary is always about *how we will react to another's behavior*, which is why it's always within our control. We can only tell someone else what we will do.

Read that part again!

We're conveying to the other person how we will behave, in advance, if they continue to act in an unwanted or harmful manner. They may not agree with us—or our characterization of their behavior. They may not agree to our stated consequences either. Doesn't matter.

What matters is the consistency of our responses.

Boundaries are not magically effective techniques that can trick someone into behaving cooperatively. They're not cleverly phrased threats that can coerce people into acting against their will. And they don't get automatic results, no matter how correctly you apply them.

Nevertheless, healthy boundaries are awesome little tools that can deliver big, life-changing results. Ready to decide to master them?

The benefits of better boundaries

Here are a few of the benefits healthy boundaries can create in your life:

- They can protect every potential area of your life: money, time, scheduling, energy, relationships, etc. Nothing is exempt.
- They protect you from the consequences and results of decisions that were made without your input.
- They allow positive elements in, while keeping harmful elements out, helping you feel safe in your environment.
- They help you exhibit (and grow) self-respect,

regardless of the level of disrespect shown to you by others.

- They help you clarify your needs, so they can be met.
- They encourage you to balance your genuine responsibilities and accept where they should be: on your shoulders, not someone else's.
- By the same token, they help you place the responsibilities that belong to others squarely on their shoulders.

Let's see what this might look like in action:

For example, perhaps in order to save your peace of mind, you can no longer be the person responsible for enforcing whether your stepchild does their household chores. He's disrespectful, doesn't want to listen to you, and you're uncomfortable enforcing consequences. You've had it. Your partner isn't happy with your decision because he works long hours and is too tired when he gets home to address the issue. But you know if you just give in and do the chores yourself, you'll end up resenting both him and your stepchild.

It may seem as if there's "no other choice" but for you to continue helping your stepchild develop a sense of responsibility, right? Yet you know this is a decision you need to make for long-term peace in your family, regardless of whether your partner agrees in the short term. To help lessen the blow, you can offer to help your partner come up with other possibilities, but don't consider that a prerequisite that you must meet first before you make a change.

As interconnected family members, we often feel anxious about "not doing our part" and are eager to provide a solution before setting a limit that's vital to our sanity. But making sure that another solution is available is not a prerequisite to instituting your boundary.

It's up to everyone involved to find an answer that works, not just you. Does that approach make you feel more hopeful? We hope so!

> **Heather G. (divorced mom, stepmom)**: *"One boundary I set was that I was not going to [custody] exchanges because she couldn't handle me there. Did I have the right to go? Absolutely. Was it worth it for me to go and have the potential of setting her off causing stress for my stepson? Nope. It wasn't letting her 'win' or have her way, it was me taking care of myself and my family."*

> **Peggy N. (divorced mom, stepmom)**: *"A huge boundary my husband and I established in our home was our reconnection time and space after work. Junior was not allowed to infiltrate our couple bubble."*

What do bad boundaries look like?

Jenna often hears clients say, "I try to create boundaries, but then she just violates them!" That tells her that her client is misunderstanding what a boundary is. Since a boundary is what you will do, others can't violate it. What they really mean is that the other person isn't honoring their request for a change.

Boundaries are this little back-and-forth dance, almost like a call-and-response part of a song that goes like this:

You	They
You communicate a boundary.	They respond with a particular behavior, likely similar to the unwanted behavior they originally had.
You impose your boundary.	They react.
You adhere to your boundary.	They respond again.

If their response is negative, repeat!

Some people think implementing a boundary means proudly taking a stand for themselves and sticking it to the other person. But once you experiment with healthy limits and consequences in your life, you'll realize that "bad" boundaries aren't even boundaries at all. The tip-offs? False boundaries are:

- Inconsistent
- Unenforceable
- Non-existent

Inconsistent boundaries

These are boundaries where your response is uneven. Sometimes you don't follow through. This results in the other person continuing the unwanted behavior because they think they can get away with it.

For example, a stepmom has agreed to communicate with the ex regarding the kids because she can communicate better than the two exes. But now and then the ex bashes the stepmom's partner. She sets the boundary, "I'm happy to communicate with you about the kids. But if you insult my partner, I'll end the conversation."

Sometimes she follows through and hangs up. But sometimes... when she's feeling that the conversation must be had, she stays on the phone for another fifteen minutes asking the ex to please stop. Her words said she wouldn't tolerate that behavior, but her actions communicate that she will randomly tolerate it. So the ex continues doing it.

Unenforceable boundaries

Lousy boundaries can also look like you're trying to control another person by telling them what to do, instead of telling them what you will do: "Stop showing up at my house." "Stop emailing me." "Don't feed the kids hot dogs with MSG in them ever again!"

These are requests or demands, not boundaries. They usually don't go over well and you can't ensure they will happen, which is why they don't work! These situations can add to your feelings of powerlessness because you're relying on the other person. If they honor your request or demand, you're happy. If not, well, bad news.

Take the example of asking your counterpart not to show up at your house without calling ahead of time. Can you really and truly keep her from ever coming over again unannounced? Even if you erected a brick wall around the perimeter of your property, can you keep her away? Can you ensure that her car will die if it comes within twenty feet of your yard? Would a small army of trained Jack Russell terriers yap her into submission? Unlikely.

But… you can tell her what you will do if she continues with her unwanted visits. "I will not answer the door if you come over without checking beforehand to see if it's a good time." And for those of you who have dealt with harassment or abusive behavior, you'll need to go a step further. "I will not interact with you in any way, shape, or form. If you continue to visit my house, I will call the police and remain inside until they arrive."

That's the difference.

Another volatile subject is social media and technology. Because of the rate of technological innovation these days, we are all experiencing an ever-increasing loss of privacy. This includes private information that the other household may choose to share with the world, such as screenshots of confidential correspondence, pictures of the children and financial information.

Unfortunately, short of continually going to court to prevent the other person's behavior, there's not much you can do about it. We know that's not the message you want to hear in a chapter on how to provide more protection in your life. But here, we'll try to keep the focus on problem-solving using consequences that are within your control. Because technology keeps changing so fast, you may have to get creative about how to formulate workable boundaries.

Non-existent boundaries

Ugh. This might feel the worst of all. Instead of asking for what you want, you bite your tongue. Instead of speaking up in the face of disrespectful treatment, you either pretend like it doesn't hurt you, try to shrug it off or assume your reaction is your problem to fix, all on your own. Perhaps instead of following up on the consequences that you told the other person to expect if they kept overstepping, you just try to avoid them and the situation, hoping it all just somehow goes away.

In the meantime, the problem continues or even gets worse. The ex-wife continues calling on the weekends after the kids' bedtime. You grit your teeth and hand them the phone, fuming, but try to smile. Or the stepmom continues to post photos of your children on social media with captions that say "Omg! My wonderful children are so silly! Never thought I could love this deeply!"

We've all been there. Here's why...

Bad instructions

It's difficult to see how we contribute to the way people treat us, and what we'll tolerate and allow. Fear and other factors can prevent us from believing we have choices, but we do.

Take a moment to think about the times you focused on the other person changing their behavior, as opposed to you changing in response to *their* unwanted behavior. Can you pinpoint where you might have taken a wrong turn and accidentally reinforced their bad behavior, or continued allowing something because of a non-existent boundary on your end?

What instructions are you creating for the other person—both spoken and unspoken?

Here's an example of accidental reinforcements:

"I sometimes respond to her, when I've already told her I won't. Even though I've set up an email filter to send her messages to a delete folder, I still check it because I'm dying of curiosity. But then I read them and get upset, then feel like I can't just let her get away with talking to me that way, so I let her know that. The drama just starts all over again."

In the words of our readers

> **Brynn (divorced mom/stepmom)**: *"I implemented a boundary with my husband's ex with her talking poorly and making jabs about my husband to me. 'I know he frustrates you, but I'm just not willing to participate in that kind of banter with you.'"*

> **Leila (stepmom)**: *"I implemented a boundary when I asked my husband's ex-wife to please keep all requests between her and my husband."*

Journal questions: How are my boundaries working?

Think of a situation where you have tried to implement a boundary, but you're still experiencing the unwanted behavior.

- What was the action you took to implement that boundary?

- Was that action focused on their actions or yours?

- In what way might have you inadvertently reinforced the unwanted behavior, like in the example below?

- Where are some areas where you suspect you have "leaky" boundaries, or perhaps even none at all?

> • What are some boundaries that have worked well for you? (Good job!)

What prevents us from creating healthy boundaries?

If boundaries are so awesome, why do we have so much trouble creating strong, clear limits with other people? For two main reasons.

First, most of us didn't grow up in families where healthy boundaries were modeled. We probably saw our mother or maternal figure bending over backwards for us and everyone around her. We saw her put her needs last and not speak up for what she wanted. Because of societal conditioning, women often feel a strong need to be liked by everyone—whether they like the other person or not. (Even if you grew up in a home where one of your parents was a narcissist and it seemed like all they did was make sure their own needs were met, that's not the same as practicing healthy boundaries, because they didn't respect you as a sovereign being with your own needs. You simply existed to serve theirs.)

Second, we're afraid of the consequences and the resistance we might encounter from other people. People can become unpredictable and aggressive when they bump up against conflicts. What happens when someone tries to tell us what we can and can't do? Many of us get defensive, thinking "you're not the boss of me!" We push back against anyone trying to dominate us, maneuvering to gain the upper hand—even if we do so later or by being passive-aggressive (an easier way to avoid direct confrontation). Teenagers know this strategy well, but so does everyone else in a contentious relationship.

So bottom line: confusion, fear, and a lack of education are major reasons women have so much trouble setting boundaries.

- Fear of saying "no".

- Fear of looking like a "bitch" or being too demanding.
- Fear of hurting someone else's feelings.
- Fear of starting conflict or perpetuating it.
- Fear of making things worse.
- Fear of creating more stress or hard work for someone else.
- Fear of not being "worth" the extra trouble.
- Fear that our loved ones won't love us anymore.

See if you recognize any of these kinds of thoughts below. These examples are based on the article *Boundaries 101: Lessons for Stepmothers* by Mary Kelly-Williams (used with permission).

Ask yourself, Am I practicing inconsistent or non-existent boundaries for any of these reasons:

To keep the peace?

"I need to be the strong one here, since I'm better at the emotional stuff than my partner."

To avoid the conflict?

"If I speak up about what I need and want, I'm just going to stir the pot and make everything worse."

To get the ex-wife or stepmom to like you?

"Maybe if I could just win her over by taking the high road and showing her what a good person I am, a lot of this conflict would go away."

To look like the good person?

"I can't stoop to her level, so I always have to seem like the nice one, the calm and clear-headed one, compared to her."

To make sure the stepkids love you?

"I just need to bite my tongue and never get mad or lose my temper. The last thing I want is to seem like a hard-ass in front of the kids. And maybe if I'm the "cool" stepmom, they'll accept me and love me."

To stay on the kids' good side?

"They've been through a hard enough time with the divorce. I'm just going to love them all the way into good health and healing as their mom, no matter what."

To be the perfect stepmother and wife?

"I'll show my husband how different I am from her. I'll show him he made the right choice in marrying me. I'll do such a great job of loving him and meeting his needs that we'll stay together. I'll show her I'm a better mother, and that I'm more caring and consistent."

To be the perfect mom and wife?

"I'll show her I know what I'm doing and that the kids will always prefer me, no matter how much she tries to be 'the cool stepmom.' I'll do such a great job with my second marriage that she'll regret being stuck with him. I'll show them both what a healthy family unit looks like, something they'll obviously never have."

To make life easier? To ensure the smooth, yet elusive "blended family"?

"If I try hard enough, I can create love, harmony and acceptance between us all."

To avoid rejection?

"If I make people mad, they won't like me anymore. I'll be shunned and left out of things."

So how does one do it? What if things go wrong? Let's walk through what's required to create healthier limits.

Enforce unpopular limits

Five steps to creating better boundaries

As you may have experienced, setting boundaries can be a complicated process even when it's broken down into steps. Let's look at each of part of the process more closely so you can do a better job of identifying where you may struggle to enforce your boundaries.

1. Identify a situation that's not working.
2. Make an initial request for a change.
3. Assess the result of your first request.
4. Communicate an action you will take if your request is not honored.
5. Respond to boundary violations with consistency and good self-care if you get upset.

1. Identify a situation that's not working

The first step to creating a boundary is identifying where it's needed. Think about everything that happens during your day. You can create a boundary around protecting your time, energy, physical space, physical belongings, and emotional wellness.

What's a situation that you're uncomfortable with or that stresses you out? That's a sign you could use a few improvements. Here are some common problems:

- Your stepchild uses your things without asking.
- Others expect you to be available without first asking.
- Disrespectful language, tone, and treatment.

- Friends and family gossip to you about others and it upsets you.
- You're expected to put others' needs above your own.
- Kids barge into your bedroom without asking.
- The other parent attempts to exert control in your home.
- The other parent insists the child keep their phone on them at all times so they have 24 hour access.
- Your stepchild exhibits disrespectful behavior to your partner, such as screaming, using foul language.

Example A: When I drop my stepson off at his mom's house, she comes to my car and insults me in a passive-aggressive way.

Example B: I have a strict policy against posting pictures of the kids on social media and the stepmom is constantly doing this without my permission.

2. Make an initial request for a change

The second step is to make a request for a behavior change. This gives the other person the option to honor your request, or ignore your request, and then experience a consequence from your actions.

It's important to remember here that the goal isn't to punish the other person. It's creating a more peaceful experience for you. We want to point this out because sometimes a boundary means removing yourself from an unhealthy situation, but it can feel like you're letting the other person win. What we want to say about that is if you're protecting yourself from an unhealthy situation by removing yourself, that's ultimately you winning. So here you'll identify what you'd like the person to do differently and then make that request. For example: Ask the ex to not communicate with you negatively when you drop off your stepson.

As much as you may not want to communicate with the other person, you must let them know you aren't happy with the way things are going and make an explicit request, asking for new behavior. A caveat to this is if you don't feel safe communicating with them, it's absolutely okay to implement a boundary, such as blocking them, without letting them know. If you're a stepmom, your partner can let the ex know that you're no longer available. If your previous interactions had nothing to do with the kids, your partner doesn't even have to inform her of your boundary.

> **Example A:** "Can you please either speak more respectfully to me when I drop the kids off at your house or not communicate with me at all?"

> **Example B:** "Could you please not post pictures of the children's faces on social media until they're at least fifteen? Thank you."

3. Assess the result

Did the person honor your request? If so, great. If not, then read on... People may react to you in one of three ways after you've made a request:

1. They accept and respect your boundary and don't repeat the same unwanted behavior.
2. They appear to accept and respect your boundary, but then attempt to cross the boundary again, hoping they'll get away with it.
3. They refuse your request and let you know they have no intention of doing as you've asked.

> **Example A:** The ex-wife refuses to see a problem with her behavior and insists that you are the one who is disrespectful.

> **Example B:** The stepmom continues posting images and updates about the children on social media and maybe even includes a screenshot of your request to her.

Of course, people with whom you have a good relationship with are more likely to honor a request for a change.

Just remember, if someone gets upset that you've created a boundary, that doesn't mean you shouldn't have. In fact, it might be further proof that you needed the boundary in the first place.

4. Communicate an action you will take if your request is not honored

It's scary to think that standing up for yourself might mean people will dislike you or see you as the "evil stepmother" or "crazy ex-wife." But if you want to succeed with healthy boundary setting, it's important that you stick to your word, even if your fears about repercussions have you shaking in your boots.

What do you want to have happen with this problem instead?

Brainstorm some potential actions you might take in response to a boundary violation. Communicate what you will do in response to the other person not honoring your request. This consists of two parts:

1. A direct request.
2. What you will do if this doesn't happen.

Use the following formula to create your boundary:

"I'd like you to (behavior change). If you continue to do (unwanted behavior), I'll do (your consequence/action)."

You do not need to engage in a lengthy conversation with the other person when you communicate your intended consequence. You don't need to get them to accept or approve of the reasons for your request. You don't need to explain your reasoning or convince them it's valid or wise. You can just inform them of your new boundary and go about your day.

> **Example A:** "I'd like you to speak to me respectfully. If you're not able to stop communicating with me in a negative

manner, I'll no longer be able to help with transportation."
(Note: In many cases, you'll be communicating this with your
partner, and they can pass it on to their ex.)

Example B: "I've asked you to honor my request, and you
have continued to post pictures of the kids. I'll have to discuss
this problem with the children's father. If we can't find some
common ground, I'll be seeking legal advice to help resolve
the issue."

5. Respond to boundary violations with consistency and good self-care if you get upset

This is where the rubber hits the road. You can expect some
pushback after you've communicated your boundary. After all,
no one likes to be told that things are going to be different from
now on. Just because you've explained what you'll do if the other
person disrespects your limits, doesn't mean you won't still get
scared and stressed out. But hold steady! Do what you said you
were going to do. You may need to repeat your own words
several times back as a reminder to yourself. It's okay to feel
anxious and off kilter here. You're doing something new and
brave, outside your comfort zone.

This would be a good time to have a friend on call, in case you
need some emotional encouragement. If boundaries are a new
concept to you and the thought of implementing them makes
you shudder, then start with a minor change, one that you feel is
easier to implement, where you don't expect as much resistance
from the other person. You can also start by creating a boundary
with someone you feel safe with. Let them know this is new for
you, you're nervous, and you'd like their support.

Example A: In this example, the pushback might be from
your partner, since he's the one who will experience the
consequence of you no longer being available to help with
transportation. You'll need to find a balance between being
empathetic to the consequences your partner will now

experience and following through with the boundary because it's what you need.

Example B: Guess what? We can't go any further with this example! That's because it's not enforceable: it's a request, not a boundary. We wanted to show you how easy it is to get misled and confused by boundaries. You could still take her to court to stop her, but that's still not a boundary because there's no guarantee it will protect you from the unwanted behavior.

Reassess your boundary periodically and fine-tune as needed

Reassess your boundary occasionally. We've encouraged you to remain firm and consistent in your boundaries, but as circumstances change, you may decide to adjust the consequences.

For example, let's say you've set a boundary with your partner that you're no longer available to get your uncooperative stepchild up in the morning. You've implemented this boundary for a while now and your partner has stepped up and has been helping their child get ready for school. One day something unexpected comes up and they ask for your assistance that morning. You may decide that you're happy to pitch in this one time. Or every now and then. That's perfectly okay.

We're not telling you to never bend, but it depends on the circumstance. Maintain your awareness and try to ensure that your involvement doesn't lead to old patterns and forgotten boundaries.

In the words of our readers

> **Jean (stepmom):** *"Respect of clear boundaries for each household works best for us, and aids in consistency and predictability of expectations for the children too, since the two households are so different."*

Meg (stepmom): *"People don't get to be mad about over-stepped boundaries if the boundary was never made clear."*

Protect your soft spots

Managing negative reactions to your boundaries

We'd be remiss if we only gave you the tools for creating healthy boundaries, but didn't provide you with a way to handle other people's reactions to those boundaries. Some common misconceptions about boundaries are that they will:

- Immediately alleviate conflict.
- Make the situation "better" for everyone involved.
- Bring about a peaceful resolution.

But the reality is that when you first implement a boundary, people are likely to be upset because you're disrupting their status quo. The boundaries are necessary because other people's status quo isn't working for you. Their grievances might include:

- It makes more work for them.
- They don't have healthy boundaries themselves so a boundary feels like rejection or betrayal.
- Your boundary interrupts a system or agreement they thought was perfectly fine.

All of these reactions could be difficult to deal with. Ultimately, you're not responsible for another person's reaction to your boundary. It's not your job to soothe the ex or try to calm her.

It gets trickier with your relationship with your partner. Although it's not your job to manage your partner's feelings, none of us want to upset our partner or be in conflict with them. This can cause us to feel guilty, or make their feelings more important than our needs and so we go back on our word. You want to find a balance of communicating your empathy to your partner, while still holding the line.

Here's an example:

"Honey, I know I offered to help with transportation, but I can no longer tolerate your ex's behavior towards me. If at some point she can leave me alone or be respectful, then I would consider helping again. I know this makes things harder on you, and I'm sorry for that. I'm happy to help you brainstorm some solutions."

1. Notice any uncomfortable feelings that are arising, such as fear, guilt, or anxiety.
2. Use one of the quick tools in Chapter One to relax your nervous system.
3. Journal about thoughts that are accompanying your feelings. For example: "I'm feeling fear that my partner will be upset with me," or "I'm feeling anxious that I helped create more drama."
   Notice any patterns that may emerge for you, such as downplaying your needs, or telling yourself it's more important to not upset anyone. Then journal about those thoughts.
4. Take one action to comfort yourself. Sip a cup of your favorite tea; take a hot bubble bath; use your favorite aromatherapy.
5. Notice if you waver or doubt if your boundary is necessary or appropriate. Now write down all the reasons you wanted this boundary in the first place. This will help to remind yourself why you need it. We can be great at talking ourselves out of something that's good for our wellbeing, especially if it upsets someone. Tell yourself that you have a right to create healthy boundaries and that it doesn't make you a bad person. You deserve to take action that improves your wellbeing, even if it upsets others.

In our experience, we've found that with our partner, the initial upset often subsides once they see how beneficial our boundary is for us. When they see us feeling happier, less stressed, and having less conflict with them, that's often enough for them to understand and accept our boundary.

In the words of our readers

J.B. (divorced mom): *"I would only answer a call or text or email if it was a direct question or communication regarding school, doctor's appointments, or anything of that sort. I would not discuss our marriage or child support (his desire to stop paying somehow entered every conversation) and I stuck to that."*

N.H. (stepmom): *"My husband's ex-wife and her husband stopped by our house and when they realized we weren't home, entered the home and sent the kids to find the Gameboys to bring along. My husband called her right away and let her know she could only come into our house when invited. She was a little upset and didn't understand why it was such a big deal. It may not have been if we'd had a different/better relationship, but she had been rude and disrespectful to me and of my boundaries in the past. Now she understands that she is not allowed in our home without our invitation."*

Sample healthy boundaries

Now that you've learned about boundaries in disguise and how to create your own healthy boundaries, we'd like to leave you with a list of examples that stepmoms and divorced moms have found helpful. Notice that each boundary is enforceable and focused on our own actions and behavior.

- Blocking the ex from social media and/or calling or texting her phone.
- Only agreeing to help with transportation if given 48 hours notice and asked if you're available.

- It's not just assumed you will be available.
- Setting a time limit on how long your partner can vent about his ex to you.
- Not being involved in drafting emails or text responses to the ex.
- Not being present at any activity the ex will be at.
- Having separate parent-teacher conferences.
- Having a landline that is the only access point for the ex.
- Politely removing yourself from the room when the extended family reminisces about the ex.

A reminder: *boundaries can be very simple.*

When another person crosses a boundary, you always have the option to either accept or reject their behavior. You can't control them, but you can always remove your participation or assistance.

Jenna has found in many of the clients she works with that a common misconception is that the women need to communicate with each other. Communication between mom and stepmom isn't necessary if it can't be respectful. Stepmoms, you are under no obligation to be the go-between or to accept communication from someone who is disrespectful to you. Your partner needs to step up and be the main communicator with their ex.

Jenna's story

Early in my career as a nurse I found myself in a situation with a person who was verbally abusive to me. I was working in a small office as a chemotherapy nurse, and my boss shared his office with his wife, who was also a doctor. After about a year, out of nowhere, my boss's wife became verbally aggressive with me and started accusing me of things I wasn't doing. Eventually, I realized my only option was to leave the job I loved, because I refused to be treated that way. I was able to extricate that person from my life, but with my partner's ex, that wasn't an option.

Once again, I thought if I could just explain myself better, be nicer, or correct her misperceptions of me, things would get better. But none of that had any effect. If anything, it just enraged her more, causing her to dig her heels in even deeper.

It became obvious to me that the only way things were going to improve for me was by creating boundaries. I blocked her from social media and, as I mentioned earlier, from my phone. If she was going to lie about me and accuse me of things I wasn't doing, I was revoking her access to me. Things got exponentially better for me from there.

Jennifer's story

I've had to learn about boundaries the hard way, after growing up knowing almost nothing about them. I've had disastrously unclear communication with my ex-husband, his wife, my husband, stepkids, my ex and his wife, and with my own children. Good times!

Expecting people to read between the lines of your hurt silences; using passive-aggressive, vague language; watering down your requests because you're afraid of asking for too much; letting things bottle up until you have an angry, loaded outburst. None of those communication habits lend themselves to cooperation, conflict resolution or feeling calm and confident.

The problem with learning about boundaries is that, initially, it's going to be ugly. You're going to be clumsy. Awkward. Your requests and responses might seem out of scale and confusing to others who wonder why you're being so weird, rigid, and wiggy.

But then… it gets better. You get used to the little communication formulas and techniques. They stop feeling so contrived and artificial. People are relieved that you're being more direct. Funnily enough, your changed behavior even gives others the freedom to ask more clearly for what they need. It all starts to feel... normal! So hang in there if this stuff is new for you. I remember those early boundary mishaps with no small amount of embarrassment. But it's all okay.

Just know that better boundaries are like a superpower in life. You're more protected from the things you don't want, but also freer to move towards what makes you happy.

Mantras for setting boundaries

- "Boundaries are how I show myself respect."
- "All healthy relationships have healthy boundaries."
- "I accept my responsibilities and leave others to theirs."
- "It's okay to say "no" to people and situations that don't support my well-being."
- "Healthy limits help stave off resentment and burnout."
- "No one gets to decide for me what my limits are."

4

INCREASE YOUR RESILIENCE

Recover / Relearn / Practice

Recover from catastrophe

Long-term neglect

Happens to the best of us: you've had enough. You're tired of trying and crying. How can you make things better? The two biggest obstacles to transforming your negative feelings are: a lack of knowledge about what to do, and having a lower tolerance to stress than you had before.

Most of us weren't taught effective self-soothing skills while we were growing up (not something our culture is really good at!) Having more of a sensitized stress response can give you the ongoing impression that you're doing a terrible job of solving problems and now need to redouble your efforts—even when you're handling challenges well.

If you've ever seen a line of trees on the coast, you'll notice that they're bent back a bit, but still able to withstand some intense wind. These trees aren't brittle or rigid. They're pliant and resilient. It's possible for us to incorporate some of those same qualities in ourselves with a little practice.

Remember that Window of Tolerance that we covered in the first chapter? Normally, we have a certain threshold for emotional triggers before we set off our fight-flight-freeze response. The lower the threshold, the more likely you are to get upset, to become overwhelmed, and to feel out of control. The higher your threshold, the greater your ability to withstand tension and conflict without going into survival mode. Not only that, you'll recover your sanity, calm, and problem-solving finesse more quickly.

But our tolerance can't change for a very important reason....

It's because we haven't had most of our needs met in a long time. We've grown used to setting aside our preferences and the things we enjoy. This starts out in small ways, such as deciding that what others in the family want for dinner is more important than what we want. Or where they want to go or what they want to watch on TV is more important than what we'd prefer. Those things are so insignificant, right?

The problem is when we defer to their wants more often than choosing our own. It adds up and can turn into us neglecting ourselves in even bigger ways, such as quitting an activity that we love, or taking part in something that goes against our values. The accumulation of these "self-sacrifices" often results in increased feelings of resentment and powerlessness, and a decreased self-esteem. We feel small and less important and can lose a sense of who we are.

This is why the practices that help you connect to yourself in this chapter are so important.

You want more for yourself than just surviving here, right? We certainly want more for you!

Bouncing back

We've listed some quick tools under the first chapter on Stress, but these are the ones to use when you need some more serious help.

A summary of our approach:

- Calm your nervous system.
- Transform unhelpful thoughts.
- Make a fresh start.

Calm your nervous system

When you're super stressed, you have an ever-ready source of support right at your fingertips. It's you, or more specifically, your body's Inner Knowing. Our body contains great wisdom. Our intuition, gut feelings and all that other internal feedback provide valuable clues about what is best for us in the moment. They also provide us with knowledge about what's missing. You can be your own best ally. Luckily, you are always there when you need someone.

If we take the time to tune inward when we're upset, we communicate to ourselves that our feelings and perceptions matter, even if it seems like they don't to other people. Our fears, our concerns, and our strongest values count. When we better understand what it is we want and need, we can make sure those things have a place at the table going forward. This is especially true when we are in active conflict with another person.

We all have an inner wisdom that is much more difficult to access throughout our busy days. But it's still there in our subconscious and in our body, even if we're ignoring it most of the time. Try this.

Exercise: What do you need and want?

Create an environment that's inviting. Light some candles, use aromatherapy or put on some soothing music. But if the best you can do is a bathroom break midday, that'll work too! Close your eyes, put one hand over your heart and one hand on your belly. Stay focused on your body, turn your attention inward, and ground yourself. Take a few slow, deep breaths. Sense what you're feeling inside your body.

1. Move from your head down to your toes if that helps, or you might notice sensations right away. Do you feel a twinge in your belly? A tightness in your shoulders? Have you been clenching your jaw? Do you have aches or pains anywhere?

2. Just notice and then make any slight movements or adjustments in your posture that feel good.

Notice if any thoughts come to your mind about what those sensations might mean. Ask your body "What would help me feel better right now? What do I need and want to feel more centered and calm? What message do you have for me?"

1. Listen. It's important that you don't make anything happen and that you don't judge yourself for whatever you experience. Connecting to ourselves is about honoring and accepting our complete self.

2. You may hear some very simple messages about next steps you need to take or even something mundane about taking care of yourself. When you're ready, open your eyes.

3. If you'd like, write down what you discovered. If you can't write anything down, no problem. Just listen to what your inner wisdom is saying. You'll remember the important parts.

Review the simple messages you heard from your inner wisdom to help them settle in your mind. Take a grounding breath or two and return to your day.

Some of you may not feel anything at first when you try this exercise, especially if you're overwhelmed. You might feel numb or very uncomfortable. That response is normal and can be from armor we've built up to protect ourselves from past hurts. Try thanking the armor for the protection it's given you, and when you're ready, let it know that you no longer need it, for now.

Ask yourself again what you need and want to feel more peaceful. If nothing comes to mind, it's okay. Accept that taking a moment to stop and slow down has still helped you reduce stress and diffuse tension.

For some of you, even taking five minutes to yourself is an accomplishment, and that's fine! Just take one small step at a time. Try sitting with yourself with some comforting music or sounds. Then commend yourself for the accomplishment!

In the words of our readers

> **Brittany (mom, stepmom)**: *"As women, we sometimes feel like we need to take care of everyone and put our needs last. I have done this many times and end up feeling resentful and irritable. When I take better care of myself, I'm able to take better care of everyone and be a happier mom!"*

> **Alanna (stepmom)**: *It's essential for our relationships that we love and accept who we are right now. It's what allows us to love and accept others.*

Transform unhelpful thoughts

Everyone has an inner dialogue that runs throughout the day. For many of us, our internal dialogue is full of self-criticism stemming from false beliefs about ourselves that were created during childhood, such as:

- "I'm not doing it right. I never do anything right."
- "I'll never be able to accomplish that. I'm not as talented as other people. It comes so easily to them."
- "I'll fail like I always do."
- "He'll never love me enough. No one will."

It's hard to feel calm and at peace when your inner monkey mind is full of blame, shame, and criticism. So let's change those messages!

First, let's help you get clear on which false beliefs might sabotage you. We want you to notice your thoughts more, instead of those beliefs operating on autopilot all day.

Turning up the volume

When you feel yourself tense up or get anxious or upset, pay attention to what thoughts are accompanying those feelings. What is your brain saying to you? Bringing those thoughts into your awareness is a gigantic step towards being able to shift them to thoughts that are true and helpful.

The simple act of noticing, "Oh, I was just thinking how I can never do anything right. Wow, is that really true? Have I never done anything right?" changes it from an unhelpful subconscious pattern to a thought that you can objectively pinpoint as untrue, and then choose to change.

We've listed some common false beliefs above, but as you pay more attention to yourself, we invite you to list the ones you most often experience below. If you're having trouble with this, notice the thoughts you use, about yourself or others, that include absolutes such as "never," "always," "impossible," "must," and "only."

What are some of your most persnickety, unhelpful thoughts?

Author Byron Katie, creator of *The Work*, has a simple yet powerful exercise to shifting your thoughts. Here's a super abbreviated version of it. For every thought you have that brings you pain, ask yourself:

1. Is that thought 100% true?
2. Who would I be without that thought?

Meditation

Meditation has been shown to have multiple benefits, from increasing your Window of Tolerance to lowering your blood pressure. There are various types of meditation, but the type we offer here consists of repeating a specific mantra, or positive affirmation. Think about what the words mean to you, and focus on how you feel when you repeat them.

Remember in Chapter 1 when you learned that your body doesn't know the difference between thinking about being in danger, and actually being in danger? Well, it also doesn't know the difference between imagining yourself at the beach and feeling at peace, and actually being at the beach and being at peace! Below you'll find multiple mantras to meditate on. Choose one or all of them. Make up your own. Experiment. The choice is yours. The goal is to find one—or several—that helps you feel calm, grounded, and inspired.

Below are basic instructions for you to follow for each meditation.

Repeating a mantra

Sit quietly in a private place where you can relax without interruptions. Soften and relax any part of your body that feels tense and tight. Take several deep, calm breaths, releasing any tension you're feeling. Bring your awareness to your heart and let your heart soften and open. Imagine yourself breathing easily through your heart. Now choose one mantra from the list we have provided below and repeat it silently or aloud.

As you repeat the affirmation, open yourself to the possibility that there is wisdom and truth in it, just waiting for you. You don't have to work hard to find it or remember it. Just know the very act of softening and opening to the words will benefit your mind and your emotions.

If you find it hard to sit with one mantra, choose another one that excites you or gives you a feeling of possibility. You can also pace or walk while you're meditating, if you feel the need to move. Some people like to break their mantra into two parts, mentally saying half the sentence on the inhale and the other half on the exhale (*I am... at peace...*).

If you're still plagued by mental chatter, simply focus on generating appreciation for all the good in your life: the people, places and experiences you love; your health; the blessings of sunlight and green grass and beautiful places in nature. Some possible mantras:

- "I am at peace."
- "This too shall pass."
- "I am safe in this moment."
- "I am strong and capable."
- "I am protected."
- "It's not about me."
- "I can handle whatever comes my way."
- "All is well."
- "I create my own path."
- "I make my own choices."

You may also want to practice using one of the mantras we have provided at the end of each chapter. These can help you transform thoughts that are specific to the sections we've covered in this book.

Make a fresh start

Sometimes, after doing all you can to attend to your nervous system and looking inward to clarify your thoughts, what you really need is just to dust off your hands and begin again. It's got two components and you get to see which one fits best for you:

1. Choose one helpful thing.
2. Wipe the slate clean.

Even when it comes to facing some of the deepest trauma of our lives, there's always the reality of needing to go and... make a sandwich, right?

This third tool is the equivalent of saying, Okay, next! New plan! It's that same feeling of shifting gears or turning the page—you get the idea. It's helpful because sometimes we need to interrupt an unhelpful pattern, such as ruminating or spinning in circles, and create a distraction for ourselves. It snaps us out of a trance and helps us course-correct.

Choose one helpful thing

Sometimes all we can handle in the moment is making the simplest choice possible. What is something we can do that will only take a few minutes to implement? Make a cup of tea? Take a walk around the block? Watch some silly animal videos? Read a few pages of a brilliant book? Scroll through Pinterest for beautiful images? Make a journal entry? Snuggle with your pet? What else can you think of?

You might decide that what you need right now is to talk to a friend. Someone who already knows the background of the problems you're facing, who knows the characters, and your fears and concerns. We'll talk more about finding the right kind of support soon, but here, we encourage you to seek out a listening ear that's compassionate, kind, and willing to help steer you towards finding a calmer resolution—not a friend who gets worked up and defensive on your behalf, or who encourages you to take impulsive action. There's a time and place for friends and family like that too. But, for now, focus on calming any volatile feelings and waiting until you're in a better place to make big decisions.

Wipe the slate clean

> "To forgive is to set a prisoner free and discover that the prisoner was you." – Lewis B. Smedes

If you're having trouble letting things go, it may be that you need to forgive yourself. Are there any words or actions that you feel bad about or regret taking? Is there something you're continuing to beat yourself up for? When we're frequently stressed, it's easy to start second-guessing our every move, thinking, *Why can't I fix this? Why didn't I handle this better? Why can't I let this stuff roll off my back?*

Forgiving yourself means you take a deep breath, focus inward and say to yourself:

Okay, reset. The mistakes I made, the things I didn't know, the good intentions that went sideways, the stuff I blew off —it's okay. I did my best. I tried. No one's perfect. I forgive myself... I am forgiven.

Then imagine all this gunk inside of you leaving your head and evaporating up into the sky and heading out into space, dissipating into nothingness, or draining out through the bottoms of your feet into the hot magma core of the earth and burning up in the fire—whatever imagery works for you. You're human. Fallible. You're going to make new mistakes even! It's okay. Accept how things went down and start all over again, fresh.

Let it be.

Forgive yourself.

The tools in this book will work best if you give yourself some grace, not hold your behavior against yourself like a harsh, judgmental critic. Forgiveness means accepting your entire self, including unkind thoughts and harmful behavior you regret.

Wiping the slate clean and forgiving yourself is not the same thing as letting yourself off the hook. That involves a whole different set of emotions, such as sheepishness, guilt, shame, and defensiveness, even anger. True forgiveness will leave you feeling lighter, emptier (in a good way), quieter, and more still. True forgiveness feels like being washed clean in a bracing river. Big difference.

From Jenna: There are many opinions about forgiveness. A popular one is that we have to forgive others in order to be free of them. In fact, I believed that for a long time—until I had a different experience. After years of trying to forgive and thinking I had, (until the next transgression and I was upset all over again), I realized that if forgiveness was a choice, I would have done it long ago.

But I don't believe it's a choice. I believe it's the result of steps you take towards healing. It's not required for healing, but healing can result in forgiveness. And I especially believe this for victims of abuse—you don't have to forgive your abuser. And you don't have to forgive to be "spiritual" and free. The pressure to forgive someone who has violated you can make you feel like a failure and throw you into a shame spiral. So here's permission to release yourself from that expectation.

Relearn default responses

Why don't we already know how to do this?

The average person isn't raised knowing how to process their difficult emotional issues. We were trained to distract ourselves, suppress our negative feelings, and generally ignore or avoid what's wrong until it hopefully goes away on its own. If you were lucky enough to have a parental figure who walked you through understanding your upsetting experiences all the way to the other side, feeling calmer and clearer, you're one of the lucky ones. But it's never too late! These skills can always be learned. If you do, you'll not only be adding some new strengths to your emotional intelligence tool belt, you'll also be changing your brain.

Here's something cool to know... Your emotional patterns reshape the future of your brain functioning. Candace Pert, a molecular biologist, proved in her groundbreaking book, *Molecules of Emotion*, that each cell in our body has over a million receptors on it for different emotions. They're like little docking stations for fear, anger, joy, excitement, etc. When you spend too much time "soaking" in one particular emotion, you strengthen the docking stations for that feeling, making it easier to experience again in the future by default. As cells divide and reproduce, they pay attention to past needs. Cells think they're "helping" by increasing the body's ability to repeat the same behavior in the interests of efficiency, such as providing more receptors for fear, since that's what it thinks you want.

Lest that fact make you feel doomed and depressed, science has also shown that with simple and deliberate retraining, your body will quickly adapt and create more docking spaces for those newer, positive feelings too. It all comes down to intention.

Become an emotional ninja

You know how intention is at the heart of successfully making any big change? You can't ignore this chapter and expect anything to change! If you do, it's like saying, "Let's clean this messy, dusty garage. But let's not take anything out of it! Let's leave the old, moldy stack of newspapers, the mouse poop over there in the corner next to the bag of birdseed with a hole in it, and the gasoline-soaked rags from cleaning up the lawnmower. We'll just move things around..."

It's going to be near impossible, right? So be inspired by those hard-working brain cells wearing those yellow safety vests, scurrying around. Let them know you want more of the good feelings, and you want more of the machinery to back you up.

Incorporate these practices into your life. Imagine how different your interactions would be if you used less emotion when dealing with someone who drives you up a wall. Instead of reacting with a judgmental tone, hurt feelings, and blame lingering in the air, you might move through the interaction with minimal damage done—to both parties. And guess what follows? The absence of repetitive internal dialogue and upset feelings.

You might even be able to move along on your merry way, feeling stronger.

Practice makes imperfect

Tidy daily

A simple, daily check keeps things from piling up and becoming overwhelming. Reconnecting with yourself and then tending to whatever you discover often leads to a greater sense of personal strength and life satisfaction, enabling you to better manage the stress you're experiencing. Having a daily practice of check-ins can help you make small but powerful changes. Then when it comes to tackling bigger challenges, you're in a better position to do so.

Daily check-in

The same exercise we covered earlier can also be done in a simplified form. Think of it as daily maintenance, like making the bed or wiping down kitchen counters. You can even do this check-in as you're doing regular household activities or while you're going about your day. The steps are pretty basic:

1. Take a deep grounding breath.

2. Turn your attention inward and scan your body and your mind.

3. How're you feeling? Scattered? Anxious? Irritated? Hopeful? Excited? Relaxed?

4. If you notice some uncomfortable feelings, see if there's anything right there, in that moment, that might help nudge you a few degrees into feeling better.

5. Then do it.

That's it! Repeat as many times as you'd like during the day.

Get good at this stuff

It's challenging to get new behaviors to stick—even if they make you feel fantastic. Isn't that weird? See if you can make them a part of your lifestyle, not just something you do when you remember. The key is to just try one of them with an "Okay, whatever. May as well…" kind of attitude and see what happens! It's like the difference between riding a bike outside in the fresh air and *reading* about riding a bike. It's in the doing that you'll really feel a change for the better in your psyche. And then, next thing you know, you'll yearn for the mental and emotional shift that you know you can get from one or more of these techniques.

Here are a few tips for incorporating these new routines and essential practices into your lifestyle, making them something you're able to do without a lot of planning. Using these exercises is like airing out your house. Start seeing these practices as part of your everyday routine, just like taking care of your surroundings. They're just as vital as showering or doing laundry. They'll make you feel together and confident.

- Create reminders to handle problems in the moment. Until these new tools become second nature, you'll need to be intentional about using them. One way to do this is to set reminders for yourself throughout the day. Keep a sticky note on the bathroom mirror, set an alarm on your phone, or wear a bracelet. What reminders have worked for you in the past?
- Get support so you can share and integrate your insights. Having outside understanding can keep your new approach front and center and makes it easier to change your behavior. Talking about your new perspective will help them become ingrained. As a bonus, you'll likely help others by sharing your own story.
- Regularly journal to show yourself the progress you're

making. When you're feeling stuck, look back at the times you were brave and bold. Remembering the times you prioritized yourself might be what you need to get back on track. It can also be helpful to see how far you've come.

Alanna (stepmom): *"In a blended family, there are so many people with different needs that it's easy to put our own needs on the back burner. But doing that only breeds resentment, anger, and isolation. We have to love ourselves enough to set aside time for self-care, so we can manage the stresses of this crazy, beautiful stepfamily dynamic."*

Peggy N. (divorced mom, stepmom): *"My me-time is a no-trespass zone. No one is allowed to infiltrate that bubble."*

Jenna's story

Growing up and until just recently, when things got rough for me, I would always be in my head. I would ruminate and try to figure out what went wrong and how to fix it. I would think, think, and think some more. Guess how many conversations with the ex I've had during a shower, where my comebacks were spot-on and left her speechless? Too many to count.

Unfortunately, that strategy only served to keep my mind on the problems and didn't give me much relief. It wasn't allowing me to recognize, much less honor, the emotions I was experiencing. It wasn't until I took a 6-month course to become a certified feminine embodiment coach that I realized how disconnected I was from my body in terms of my emotions.

Now, one of the most effective tools I have to process stress in general, but especially the crazy things I experience as a stepmom, is tuning into my body. I immediately place my focus there and on what I'm feeling. I don't judge it as good or bad, right or wrong, I just notice it. I feel those feelings and emotions in my body and acknowledge them until they pass. Which they always do.

Jennifer's story

The funny thing about getting older is that some of the stuff you used to blow off, power through, or power lift catches up with you. Whether it's letting things pile up that I've put off, or pushing back sleep because I miss having more downtime to myself in the evenings, I have seen that I have to make self-care a priority or I'll regret it. Especially now that I have a few new health problems that I didn't used to have.

Like Jenna, I too try to use my body's signals as a type of early warning system, just like for weather forecasting. If I find my heart rate going up, fatigue creeping in or the feeling of stress in my jaw or throat, I try to pay attention and do something simple and practical about it. Sometimes that means I sit down for a few minutes for a brief rest. It might mean getting out of the house for a hilly walk, or it could mean I need to reconnect with someone I love and send a text or hop on the phone.

Whatever the case, my whole life goes a lot smoother when I remember to monitor my inner state more closely and take care of myself, just like I would a young child or a puppy. So love your inner puppy! Or kitten, if you're a cat person.

Mantras for resilience

- "My needs are as important as everyone else's needs."
- "Taking care of myself is not selfish or self-indulgent."
- "When I take time to recharge, my whole family benefits."

- "I pause to look inward and tend to my own healing."
- "Feelings are not good or bad, they are just comfortable or uncomfortable."

5

CHOOSE YOUR ROLES

Expectations / Responsibilities / Limits

Clarify your expectations

Hostile job-sharing

Roles in blended families are the stuff of legendary battlefield skirmishes. You're on the hook for a job you might never have wanted or no longer want. There's no end date to your tasks. Perhaps hardest of all, your performance review might be conducted by someone who dislikes you... or even a child!

After a divorce, roles are all up for reinterpretation, with each household forming their own rules. But now there are two matriarchs with their own realms. Two ladies of the house. Two heads of the household in competition for a role that is supposed to be theirs and theirs alone.

Imagine showing up to work one day and being told, "Morning! Guess what? You're now sharing your job with (insert name) here! You'll both be on the hook for whatever results you deliver, so you'd better do a great job. Best of luck! You're on your own, so figure it out!" All of this, while your work companion glares at you from behind the boss's back.

Moms often feel as if the other woman is trying to fill her shoes. Stepmoms often feel as if they have all the pressures of responsibilities of motherhood, but none of the power.

Out of thin air

Remember how emotional authority influences our behavior with those we love? Now, there are likely two family units that are working against each other. One marital relationship is more important to its members than the other (or the single parent, if unpartnered). Children may have three, four, or more authority figures in their lives.

Every family unit has their own beliefs and expectations. The problem is, we arrive at these beliefs without a lot of conscious thought. We just do things a certain way because that's how we've always done them. That's what seems normal. Our assumptions about how to be are nonverbal, tacit, seemingly permanent, and not updated when situations change.

Romantic anticipation of needs

Remember what it's like when you first fall in love? Your brain is swimming in a lovely chemical cocktail of euphoria in the initial stages of a romantic relationship. It feels great to anticipate your partner's needs—to provide for them without being asked, just for the pure delight of pleasing them. But this behavior plays out differently for both women after divorce and remarriage.

Stepmoms in particular might feel initially happy to step in without prompting and pick up the slack for their busy partner. Their primary intention is to be helpful, but sometimes there's also a subconscious motivation of trying to solidify their place in the family unit. Their partner might unconsciously assume that some tasks associated with running a household or caring for children should be done by her, particularly if his job seems more demanding or if he makes substantially more money (which is often the case in this day of pay disparities).

If a stepmom has kids of her own and was used to being in charge in her own home, it can be quite a shock to feel demoted, like she's now fallen several notches down the power totem pole. She may even find herself caught in a terrible bind where she is devoting more of her life energy to pleasing her partner and prioritizing his children over her own. If she doesn't have kids, she may feel like she comes in second place behind the kids, who have needs that cannot be ignored. That earlier feeling of her partner stopping the world to focus on her may be pretty short-lived.

For moms, that reliable, primal bond with the father is now gone. Even if the mother was the one who initiated the divorce, she may still have some expectations about the father's involvement in the children's lives. Whether she is a single parent or remarried, it seems normal for her to keep that old feeling of control as the family matriarch. Having another woman in the picture throws a wrench into everything. Even if a divorced mother remarries, she may find herself in a position where it seems like she's the only one responsible for "dealing with her kids," while her new husband stays out of it and reserves most his energy for his relationship with her.

That heady, romantic chemical cocktail can help explain how we got ourselves into this mess of taking on a role we now hate and wish we could change. You may have never even asked yourself in the beginning of your new family life, Do I want to do these things? In trying to be super helpful or responsible, we might not have consciously chosen the responsibilities we ended up stuck with. But it's never too late: we can make a conscious choice now.

The raw material of expectations

If the expectations we have in our lives are like movie scripts we're playing out, imagine all the "shoulds" and "have-tos" and "you betters" we're obeying. Imagine your partner's. And the children's. And the other household's!

If you think you don't have any unspoken dual-family rules, look at the following list and see what springs to mind. What assumptions did you have when you first became involved in your particular situation?

Moms, what expectations did you have regarding:

- Your emotional response to your ex-husband remarrying?
- The type of woman he would marry?
- Your co-parenting relationship when he remarried?
- How your children would respond to his new wife?
- The impact your children's stepmom would have on you and your life?
- Her involvement with school, doctor's appointments, other parents, etc.?
- How you might feel protective of your children when your ex has children in his new marriage?

Stepmoms, what expectations did you have regarding:

- The difficulty or ease of transitioning into a stepfamily?
- What your marriage would look like?
- The level of closeness you'd feel toward your stepchildren?
- The level of acceptance you would receive from:
  ○ Your extended family?

- ○ Your husband's extended family?
  - ○ Schools, doctor's offices, other parents, etc.?
- The impact your husband's ex-wife would have on you and your life?

You get a divorce and stay single, or start a new relationship. You fall in love with a father with kids. Next thing you know, "somehow" you find yourself performing the same repetitive tasks, some of which you're okay with—and some you are not.

What's more, you are regularly butting heads with the other household over repetitive behaviors that you find confounding! Take a look at some unspoken expectations below and imagine how differences of opinion in these areas might play out.

Moms

- "My ex should still fix things around our house that I can't, since it's expensive, he knows I can't afford it, and it's for the kids' benefit too."
- "He should listen to me vent about the kids' bad behavior because he's their father and needs to know what's going on with them."
- "The stepmom should never reprimand my children, only their father. She doesn't know about their personalities, sensitivities, or deeper issues."
- "The stepmom should not be picking up the slack for their father's lack of involvement. It only perpetuates the problem."
- "If the stepmom wants to be the maternal figure, then she should help them clean up."
- "Their father should remind them about their chores, not the stepmom."
- "If the stepmom loves my kids so much, she shouldn't be so happy to get them out of the house."

Stepmoms

- "My opinion and concerns should take priority over his ex's now, since he's no longer married to her."
- "He shouldn't do what she wants over what I want, just because my upset is easier to resolve than hers."
- "Maybe my partner doesn't think it's important that his kids have chores or learn responsibility. But if I don't do it, the house will always be a pig sty and I'll be upset, so I'll choose the lesser of two evils."
- "I'll fix the children's unacceptable behavior by healing them with a loving, nurturing household, with good meals, a clean environment and steady, reliable caretakers. I can transform them."
- "It's the mom's fault that the children aren't better behaved, not my husband's, so I'm going to let that be her problem to fix as much as possible."
- "A good mom should never talk negatively about her child's father."
- "A good mom should always be on time to her child's activities."
- "If the mom loves her kids so much, she shouldn't be so happy to get a break from them."

It's not just the adults who are blindly playing out their assumptions, it's the kids too. Some examples of children's expectations might include:

- "Mom or dad (or the stepmom or stepdad) will do this for me, even though I could probably learn how to do it myself. This way is just easier."
- "I will not take their threats or requests seriously because I never had to before."
- "I see the chance to gain some new power here by making people upset!"
- "I will be the "good" child and get approval and attention by chipping in, being cheerful, and never

acting up, even when I'm sad or angry."

Define real responsibilities

Determining who does what

Now that we know more about unspoken expectations, it's time to take a closer look at what we're actually doing. What are the nuts and bolts of the tasks you're expected to manage with parenting, partnership, and housework?

You might be so busy doing that it's been a while since you stepped back and thought about whether these areas of responsibility need to be rebalanced. So here's your chance to reassess. In the next section of this chapter, we'll tell you how to reassign the tasks that no longer work for you.

If you were to make a list for all the jobs you have as a single parent, remarried parent, or stepmom, what would be on your list?

Remember, think: Parenting, Partnership, and Housework.

Unconscious agreements

Does your list include tasks you didn't realize you were signing up for, but are now stuck doing? Are you performing "kindnesses" out of obligation? Are your actions fear-based or are they done from generosity? Are you making an unspoken "trade" of sorts? That broken sense of belonging we described earlier is a powerful motivator to keep giving, to keep stretching, and to err on the side of generosity.

So many actions that start from love can somehow backfire. Then, before we know it, we've created a sense of entitlement for our children, stepchildren, and our partners.

We fear creating the space to let others do their duty as self-respecting, responsible family members (even a five-year-old can put their dirty dishes in the dishwasher or fold towels from the dryer, although maybe not very well!) because we don't want to seem selfish, petty, uncaring or, god forbid, not maternal enough.

We yearn to take a moment for ourselves or delegate responsibilities, but pay a steep price for it in resentment and guilt. The hamster wheel starts up in our heads as we complain to ourselves that other people should help more, or doing what they're supposed to for their allowance, or how you have too much already on your shoulders. Then you move from that to thinking about how you want your children or stepchildren and your partner to feel like their house is a home, full of nurturing and warm energy and "the little extra touches." So you decide, "Well, just this once, since they're having a rough week or a bad day..."

And it continues.

Chosen roles (ones you're happy to take on)

With so many potential problems, it's also important to remember that there are likely many responsibilities you're happy to have and anticipate continuing to do. That's great! These are things you're good at, other people are happy they can rely on you and it brings you satisfaction, joy, and a deep sense of purpose to contribute to your family in these ways. As you repeat the repetitive tasks of family life, your routines bring you a sense of comfort and joy. Your work is the visible manifestation of love. You take pride in your consistency, patience, and adaptability. It's good to recognize these responsibilities too so you can keep the good things and the things you want to change in perspective.

A note about "taking off the parenting hat" when the kids leave. For stepmoms, it's common to feel a sense of relief when you get a break from the kids. Some stepmoms jump for joy at the break because they're dealing with disrespectful stepchildren or are simply overdoing. Others miss their stepkids, but still savor being able to attend to other things, like time with their partner, or their own child. This can be challenging because most fathers miss their kids when they're gone. Stepmoms can feel guilty when they're relieved, but their partner is filled with grief.

Moms can have the same mixture of feelings when their kids go to their dad's house. Whether they're single parents or remarried, it's wonderful to get a break and feel like parenting duties in your house aren't resting only on your shoulders. Of course, moms may miss their children. But just as with stepmoms, it's nice to have more time and space to catch up, focus on other priorities, spend time with your partner, friends and family, and maybe even date.

Exercise: Clarifying my tasks

Now, it's time to look at *all* the things that you're doing in your daily life. So grab a piece of paper and a pen.

1. Review the list earlier in this section listing the common parenting, partnership, and household responsibilities for stepmoms and divorced moms. Copy the items on the list that fit for you. Add tasks we've missed, especially ones that drive you crazy.

2. For each item, notice if it is a task that you just "slide into," or if it's a conscious choice that you still feel good about.

3. Mark unconscious agreements with a UA. Mark conscious choice with a CC.

4. After you've completed your review, place a star next to the top three responsibilities you'd like to change. We'll be focusing on these next.

5. Store your responses in a safe, private space where you can easily retrieve them.

Set empowering limits

Feminine martyrs, overdoing

As women, we constantly try to anticipate what people need and do it before being asked, either as a show of love or perhaps because we feel pressured to fill a societal role. But what are the consequences? Well, because of all these extra tasks we've taken on, we're exhausted and we—and the people around us—suffer because of it. Doing too much for others is a strong symptom of a lack of boundaries. It leads to feeling taken advantage of and breeds ongoing, accumulating resentment.

Here are some ways *both* women often overdo with parenting, partnership, and household chores:

- You make breakfast for everyone, without help from anyone else who's old enough to do it.
- You shuttle kids off to school and it makes you late to work when they're fully capable of walking themselves.
- You make dinner and are the only one who ever cleans up the dishes or pots and pans.
- You constantly pick up socks and underwear and wet towels from the floor.
- You do everyone else's laundry and put it all away, alone.
- You clean the kids' bedroom, no matter how old they are.

In Gary Chapman's book, *The Five Love Languages*, one of the love languages he describes is "Acts of Service." People who fall under this category feel loved when someone completes a task for them and they show their love for others this way as well. Acts of service are a common love language for men, as they are natural providers and it feels good for them to do for their families by making a living, repairing things around the house, fixing a problem, etc.

But for women, they're sometimes giving for other reasons, such as the things that our society values. Examples of this are stepmoms who often help their partners because they have something to prove: that they're a wonderful homemaker and a better wife than the ex. Moms may also have something of their own to prove: that they can do it all themselves or show the stepmom how much better they are at relating to the kids. Instead of following these societal scripts, how can you use a positive mindset to set you and your family up for success?

The answer: You must give away some of the responsibilities you've taken on.

How overdoing "from love" can backfire

You may justify your mile-high list of responsibilities by saying, "Hey, I'm tough. I can take it. I'm knowingly working this hard and I accept it. Plus, I want to show the kids what true responsibility looks like." But consider what you might be taking away from other people. Even though we have the best of intentions, here are some ways in which overdoing makes us (and others) crash and burn:

- You're taking away people's opportunities for growth and increased responsibility. Everyone needs to feel capable and competent. It's often through challenges and discomfort that we grow the most, feeling our way into new skills through failure, trial and error. Just because your husband, stepchild, young child, or teen is lousy at something and you can do it "right" doesn't mean you should. When will they get any better if you're always stepping up and doing it for them?
- The men in our lives long to feel useful, like their contributions mean something to us. But if we're doing

everything for ourselves and everyone else, our partner may think he's not needed. He may react by shutting down or ceasing to offer his help in the future.

- All your overdoing may offend the other woman. In fact, she might be insulted because she thinks you're trying to make her look bad. Sure, those are her insecurities at play, but by doing less you both win.
- There's a price you and your family pay for doing everything. Your energy is zapped. You're cranky. Everyone "expects" things of you now because that's what you've taught them to expect. You have no time for you. Perhaps your family has noticed you've been on edge lately and are losing your cool at the drop of the hat. They're walking on eggshells around you.

Just like what can happen with a high-stress job, burnout requires a special mention. You may reach a point in your family life where you've just hit your limit. You've run out of steam; everything makes you angry or sad or maybe you just feel numb. You've lost your motivation to try and you'd pay good money to run away from it all and live in a shack by the ocean or alone in the woods. You can't parse out what needs to change anymore, what works, and what is killing your soul.

Burnout is serious because it means you have reached a crisis point and change is urgently needed. It can cause you to catastrophize your current situation, make rash decision and lash out when you normally wouldn't.

The good news is, *recognizing that you're suffering from burnout can help you.*

It lets you know you're on a predictable path that many other women have traveled—and come out the other side, happier, healthier and more balanced. Reaching this flash point means you can take stock, address the aspects of your family that aren't working, and make some adjustments to feel better about your life.

Balancing my responsibilities

Whether you'd rate your stress as occasional or precariously unstable, let's talk about how to create more balance in your role.

Go back to the list you made earlier with all of your daily and weekly tasks under Clarifying My Responsibilities. Where are you struggling with responsibilities that are genuinely yours?

What tasks do you detest doing? Are you willing to "trade" any jobs? Is someone else in the family better at certain chores than others?

What were you initially hoping to gain or achieve by taking on this responsibility? (your first response might be, "a clean house," but dig deeper to see if there's anything else there.)

Exercise: Your responsibilities review

1. Grab the list of your responsibilities with daily and weekly tasks.

2. Go through each item and note whether you love it (L), hate it (H), or feel neutral about it (N)

3. Then choose one of the "hate" items and brainstorm some alternatives to the task by answering some questions:

    Who else can do it?
    Can you do it less frequently? Take turns? If the task has to fall on your shoulders right now for whatever reason, can you craft a transition plan to hand it off to someone else? Can the task be removed altogether?
    Whose responsibility is it truly?

The list of items above where you're overdoing is a goldmine. Really! The stuff you hate most in your family life is now going to become the raw material of change and improvement—instead of expectation, overwhelm, and resentment.

Some deeper questions to ponder…. What do you want and

need to let your partner, the other parent, the stepkids, or your children do? Where are their areas for growth and increased responsibility? Where are you taking away from them by doing for them?

What does it mean to you if you stop overdoing? Are you afraid of pushback, negative reactions or the potential discomfort of upsetting people?

Let's learn more about how to put your changes into practice.

Three ways to stop overdoing

Once you've gotten a clarity on specific tasks, here's how to go about making a change. There are three primary techniques that will help you stop overdoing:

1. Create a workaround to minimize the negative consequences of someone who doesn't want to cooperate with you.
2. Delegate.
3. Go on strike.

1. Create a workaround

This tool requires a bit of creativity and thinking outside the box. If your partner will help you brainstorm the workaround, even better, since it'll be much easier to implement if you have their buy-in.

Choose just one item from your Hate list above.

Then, ask yourself: If you could peek into a crystal ball and see that despite every single effort of yours, this situation never worked out as is, how would you save yourself the trouble of all that wasted effort? What would you do? If it helps, sit down with a piece of paper and write every idea that comes to mind, no matter how crazy (but nothing violent or illegal, of course). You might surprise yourself with some practical ideas that aren't too hard to implement.

Here's a common example: You cook dinner for the family every night, which includes your children and stepchildren. The older children complain about what you make, sometimes scoop it into the trash after a few bites, and don't help clean up. You're tired of trying to please people and washing pots and pans alone, putting away leftovers and wiping down the messy table.

Some potential workarounds, no matter how wacky:

1. Tell the kids they will each cook dinner one night a week. They get to make whatever they want and you will do the grocery shopping, but they alone are responsible for all the cooking and cleaning—and making something that appeals to people!

2. Alternatively, post a meal list on the fridge and ask people to sign up for particular dinners in advance. If they join in, they have to help clean up. If not, they must make something healthy for themselves and leave not a crumb or dirty counter behind, or lose a privilege, such as use of a device.

3. Surprise the kids by only cooking dinner for yourself and your partner. Tell everyone else it's just too hard to keep making meals only to see them tossed out, so you just gave up. Oops.

4. Once a week or month, have a cooking contest with one child, or two cooking together, or maybe even teams of the girls against the boys. If they make a meal where they get a thumbs-up from everyone, they win a silly prize or get paid for their efforts!

Take some time to list the situations in which you'd like to find workarounds. Then brainstorm the possibilities.

If you're still having trouble figuring out potential workarounds for a problem that's driving you up the wall, here's one more creative tactic. If someone was going to pay you a million dollars to solve this problem without getting anyone else to change and guaranteeing that you'd be happier, what would you do?

2. Delegate

Feeling stuck? Not sure how to delegate to others? Try out these steps below. If you can delegate just one task, that's a great start. Baby steps are okay here.

The more you share the load, the more comfortable you'll get. As your stress level decreases, your entire family will benefit.

Exercise: Decide which tasks to delegate

1. Review the items on your list from earlier in this chapter and note the tasks you'd like help with.

2. Next to each action, write down who normally completes that task.

3. Now go through the list again and look at which tasks have your name next to them. Assign each task a score, 1 for tasks in which it is absolutely necessary for you to be the one completing it, and 10 for the tasks that could easily be given away to someone else in the family, especially if it falls under "Great Life Skill to Have."

4. Beginning with the 10s, start assigning them to different family members.

5. Continue delegating your tasks until you get to a place where you're comfortable and don't feel so overwhelmed with the amount of responsibility on your plate. Experiment!

Sounds easy enough, right? But how do you ask loved ones for help?

For those of you who aren't very confident in your communication skills, we offer some sample language for requesting changes and delegating. It's hard to ask for what you need. Sometimes seeing an example helps you envision what it might look like or sound like for you to do it. Here are some ideas:

"Honey, I know we've all been really stressed lately. Can we sit down and talk about how possibly rearranging some of our responsibilities might help with that?"

"Honey, I'm feeling overwhelmed right now. I'd like to look at some alternatives to me picking up the kids from school one or two days a week. Freeing up that time for me would really decrease my stress level and would provide me with the ability to better support you and the rest of the family."

"Kids, since you're getting older, it's time for you to take on more responsibility. Here is a list of things that keep our household running smoothly. Can each of you choose one that you want to be responsible for?"

3. Going on strike

Sometimes, the best thing you can do is to just stop performing a task and leave a space there for someone else to fill, even if that means that it stays empty for a while and creates problems for others that make them angry. Plenty of women have "gone on strike" with effective results.

Sometimes we need to step back so others can step up.

You're not an indentured servant for life who can never change your role. You're allowed to say no and renegotiate your responsibilities, even if it pisses other people off and makes their lives harder.

If you're feeling nervous about this approach, it might help to remind ourselves again of the opportunities we are taking away from others to keep ourselves on track in this area. We can also hold up a positive vision of one of the most important goals we have in our divorced families and stepfamilies: to turn our young, impressionable children into skillful, competent adults who take pride in themselves. If we're going to help our children mature, then we must learn how to step back, so they can do more.

We encourage you to practice great self-care to recuperate from the conflict you're experiencing with others in the process, particularly if it's happening in your own home, which makes it harder to escape. Be gentle and kind with yourself. Remind yourself that all things must pass. And get some significant support from understanding, helpful friends, which is what our next chapter is all about!

In the words of our readers

We asked our readers: what "shoulds" do you believe in? How do they differ from how the other household behaves and what actually happens? Here's what they said:

> **Amanda D. (mom, stepmom):** *"Stepkids should have a set bedtime schedule during the week while in school. They should not stay up until 12:30 or later on a school night. They need their rest to be at their best in school, no matter their age, but especially in junior high and lower grades."*

> **Heather G. (divorced mom, stepmom):** *"My stepchild's mom should let my husband parent on his own time as he sees fit (unless it will harm the child, and even that is subjective). When two parents separate, they lose control over what goes on in the other house. The faster they accept that, the better it is for them."*

> **Jean (stepmom):** *"Each parent should be fully responsible for the children and parent their own way during their parenting time."*

> **Lauren T. (stepmom):** *"Parents and stepparents should be respectful toward all involved caregivers of their child; whether it be an ex, a stepparent, an in-law, etc."*

> **A.M. (divorced mom, stepmom):** *"My stepchild's mom shouldn't feel entitled to know everything that goes on in our house, shouldn't feel entitled to comment on every little thing in a negative way or tell the kids what they can and cannot do at our house."*

K.K. (mom, stepmom): *"Parents should put their own feelings aside to ensure that the children have a great relationship with each parent."*

Trish D. (divorced mom, stepmom): *"Parents should never tell a child to keep a secret from their other parent. This just sets the kid up to be vulnerable to predators."*

Jenna's story

One thing that I remember so clearly when I first met my husband was thinking that his kids were 9 and 12, so they were "already raised." I was childless by choice, so I thought at their ages I'd have little child-rearing to do. I laugh now at how naïve I was. Sure, I wasn't tucking them into bed at night, but I was still a caregiver. I was still taking care of them in other ways, at least when their mom wasn't trying to block me.

My oldest stepson struggled with addiction, so our lives consisted of psychiatric evaluations, hospitalizations and rehabs, overdoses and nights we didn't know where he was. As a Registered Nurse, I had insight into the medical field. I knew what questions to ask doctors and aspects of the situation that my husband just wouldn't know without having the professional training and experience I had. I wanted to support him in that way. I wanted to help the kids in that way. But most of the time, his ex would not allow it. So although that made it harder on everyone, I helped as much as I could from the sidelines. Sometimes my husband would set up separate calls with the doctors and the school. Other times I'd write a list of questions for him to ask the psychiatrist about the medicine we had to administer.

I find it so sad for the kids that some parents can't just allow other adults to care for their kids in a way that most benefits the kids. But that's just the reality for many stepparents. And so, sometimes we have to get creative and help as best we can within the confines of our given situation. For me, I realized I had the freedom to interact with the kids the way I wanted to when they were in my house. I could laugh with them and be curious about their lives and I could be there for them when they wanted to share something they didn't want to share with their parents. Being present like that paved the way for a closer relationship with them. And I believe being that person for them had a greater impact than being involved in talking to their teachers and doctors.

Jennifer's story

Oh my god, what was I thinking? When my husband and I were first dating, we both waxed nostalgic about our grandparents and how straightforward their roles were as the breadwinner and the homemaker/mother. Somewhere in the back of my mind, I thought I would be the keeper of the hearth, making meals and keeping a cozy, nurturing house alongside my writing projects. I also assumed that providing such a steady, soothing environment would make family life just gel, helping us all to avoid some of the typical blended family problems. Ha! Life had other plans. So did the people I lived with, who had no interest in the food I was making (That smells weird. It's making me nauseous.), cleaning up the common areas at the end of every day (Why can't I just leave this here if I don't care where it goes?) or creating a new holiday ritual (But this is what we've always done on Halloween!). Over and over again, I felt unappreciated, resentful, and like I was just plain worn out from all the head-butting.

Living in a blended family offers countless "spiritual opportunities" to let go of your expectations, so they can scamper off the road into the bushes before being mowed down by a speeding car. I had to learn that despite our earlier vision of domestic bliss, everyone had their own ideas about how they wanted things to be. Sure, as the adults in the room, it was our job to lead the way. But if we wanted anyone to follow, we had to make them feel included and valued too.

Mantras for clarifying your role

- "My role does not define me."
- "I'm allowed to love or not love my stepchildren."
- "I can hand over responsibilities that are not mine and still be a good parent and partner."
- "I get to decide for myself how I will show up for my family."
- "Perfection doesn't exist, but good enough does."

6

HELPFUL OR HARMFUL SUPPORT

Advice / Comfort / Wisdom

Become an advice detective

"But I'm trying so hard!"

We seek help for conflict with the other woman because it's so confusing and impacts so many areas of our life. But are you getting the support you need—or just the kind you want?

You may, in fact, simply be needing someone to acknowledge your pain and the difficulties you're facing. Or, you may be in dire need of some intense brainstorming and a fresh perspective to resolve the challenges tripping you up. We get into trouble when we're not aware of what kind of support we need and end up with the wrong one.

For example, let's say it's been a while since you've been able to express yourself and the difficulties you're having. When the opportunity presents itself, perhaps on social media or with a group of friends, you purge all your pent-up emotions. Afterward, you'll probably feel lighter. It's good to get that out of your system. But it's possible later in the day you'll feel even worse than before. Maybe it turns out that the vent session just fed your obsession with the situation and now you're even more indignant. What you might have needed was someone to help you come up with steps you could take to resolve or better manage a specific situation. But instead, you just got a bunch of people telling you you're right and agreeing that your situation is awful.

Our goal in this chapter isn't to determine who's right or wrong in your situation. It's helping you create an honest, effective support system for your mom/stepmom problems—one that gets you some place that's good for you over the long run.

What does support really mean?

We're looking for three main components when we're struggling and seeking help: sympathy, understanding, and agreement. But each of these elements can be a double-edged sword. They can calm and comfort—or lead us down a self-defeating road.

Here are the positive aspects of support:

Sympathy

Friends and family members are rooting for you. They are on your team. If someone has wronged you, your listener is irritated on your behalf. If you're hurt, they're concerned. If you're scared, they'll reassure you.

Understanding and familiarity

Friends and family get it. They know who's involved, the backstory, and most of the relevant details. You can speak in "shorthand" and they instantly understand what's at stake and what options you're considering.

Agreement

Friends and family echo your own words back to you, aghast at the stupidity, insensitivity or bad intentions of the other person. They bolster your sense of feeling rightfully hurt or angry as you vow to take action, show the other side how it's done, or prove that you're the "better person." In many ways, "the other side" is automatically the villain, no matter their motives, fears, or concerns.

The benefits of a healthy, truth-telling support system

It's in your best interests to vent your emotions with care, but also choose the feedback you trust with discernment. Balanced support is based on honesty and compassion. That kind of support gives you some wonderful gifts because it:

- Helps you illuminate your blind spots and see the big picture.
- Helps you tell the truth about your unhelpful actions and why you might have behaved this way—you can then do the same for her behavior, which depersonalizes it and makes it feel less threatening.
- Is shorter, quicker, and more powerful than the long stories involved in being a victim.
- Makes it easier to forgive yourself and forgive others (if that feels right for you).

Most of us have a mish-mash of healthy and unhealthy

relationships in our lives—whether with our family or friends we've had for years. Old patterns of behavior with our people can feel sustaining and reassuring, but also short-sighted and entrenched. If some of your sources of support could use a little freshening up, then read on!

Rate your different sources of validation

How are your current attempts to solve your most pressing problems working? Think of specific friends and family, co-workers, and websites or online forums where you are an active participant or reader. Mark an X in the column that best describes how you feel after receiving support from that person or group.

	Validated. I have new ideas that help me feel empowered and hopeful.	Validated. They get it and that's all I need right now.	Validated. But worse. Angrier or more upset than ever.	Invalidated. Not understood, all alone and more hopeless.
Family				
Friends				
Online Support				
Co-Workers				

Any surprises? What did you discover as you thought about this issue more deeply?

In the words of our readers

Annie (stepmom): "*My biggest problem with many stepmom 'support' groups: my little problem grows as everyone else dumps their own issues onto mine. When I stopped venting to people and just dealt with the issues privately instead, there was a lot less stress,* *a lot fewer voices in my head. I could deal with the mom and only the mom, not the ghosts of the other 'evil moms' as well."*

K.K. (mom, stepmom): *"Talking to people who won't call you on your part in things and only see things from a similar perspective is not helpful. I found the more I moaned about my stepchild's mom, the angrier and more unhappy I got, to where I lost myself in it all."*

A word about family

Family can be a great support system, but your stress can also weigh on them. It's difficult for them to see how much pain you're in. They want you to feel better now. They want you to be "right." They want you to "win." And although these are feel-good sentiments, they're not necessarily going to bring you peace. They're also probably pretty biased.

Family is also likely to hold your complaints against the other party. What if one day you work it out? It might be much harder for them to forgive the other party than for you. Of course, we're not saying never turn to family for support. We're just asking you to consider the potential consequences and be judicious with what you share.

Deep comfort

The consequences of agreement-only support

If you have your own team of Yes Friends, nodding their heads as you explain your tale of woe, you're potentially missing out on one of the most valuable perspectives of all. It may be the answer to your problems—but it's also one you can't see! Trouble is that your listener can't see that fresh perspective either.

This is because most advice is not objective. It's created by each person's personal opinions, experiences, their own patterns of behavior, shortcomings, unconscious beliefs, and old baggage. They're likely projecting previous negative experiences onto your situation, which can be terrible for helping you create nuanced, complex insights. If you and your friends don't understand important elements of your situation, then for that very reason, their advice is incomplete and harmful, sending you off in the wrong direction.

In addition, creating and perpetuating drama gives our nervous system an adrenaline hit that can take a toll on us over the long run. It can even become addictive, especially if you're dealing with a high-conflict person. Initially, you might just be confused about why they don't want to get along with you. But then, after you keep running into the same walls and getting more frustrated and indignant, the problems start to just seem inevitable, along with your reaction to them. Keep in mind that everybody is at risk for seeking this kind of drama-adrenaline hit. Even you and your friends. So although we all do this from time to time, if you can recognize the temptation, you'll be able to choose different actions, instead of ones that keep you stuck.

It is comforting to have people agree with you and your experience. We all need to be validated now and then. We just want you to realize that's what may be happening, and not confuse it with problem-solving, moving-forward support.

Here are the cut-and-dried consequences of seeking agreement-only support:

- Limits new perspectives: Instead of opening your mind to other ideas and actions that might resolve the conflict, you're now stuck reinforcing your current way of thinking and patterns of behavior.
- Backs you into a corner: Rather than deal with the mess and ambiguity of reality, where you admit your mistakes and make amends, you feel compelled to stick to your black-and-white story with no shades of grey. Friends and family expect this as well.

- Keeps you accountability-free: On the surface, it seems like a good idea to blame others. We remain the victim, always in the right, while others play the villain. This sympathy loop keeps you powerless and upset since you must generate fresh problems to keep a constant supply of commiseration.
- Feeds into a cycle of negativity: The only people who like to hear others complain without taking steps to fix the problem are people who are just as miserable. If you've ever thought "What has become of me? I never used to be this negative. I'm even a little sick of me!" then it's time to change your tune.
- Encourages you to distort the truth: There's a good chance you're not telling the whole story when you're working from the Land of Heightened Emotions. This is a friendly way of saying you may be (cough) exaggerating (cough) the facts, or conveniently leaving a few important details out. Like the consequences listed above, this shrinks your available options. You also have to stick to a particular "version" of events, which can be hard to remember!

Journal questions: My support comfort zone

Can you relate to the list above?

- What are some experiences in your past where you sought unhealthy support?

- Did you ever seek help and have it go surprisingly well?

- What was the difference?

What healthy support looks like

In the former No One's the Bitch (NOTB) community, many people report that it's hearing from the perspective of "the other woman" that has most opened their eyes and helped them let go of their anger, resentment, hurt, and fear. They hear opinions they might never have considered had they listened to their regular sources of input and support. Don't get us wrong. We're not saying that a different perspective justifies destructive behavior, but it can bring you a new level of understanding and clarity that helps you let go of damaging emotions.

If you want to get through the challenges of your dual-family problems with your sanity intact, you'll need good friends who will tell you the truth, even when you don't want to hear it. Friends and family who will put themselves in the uncomfortable position of potentially making you angry, hurting your feelings, wounding your pride, or eliciting an adverse reaction with that honesty. In doing so, they're taking a risk. But ultimately, you can trust their actions come from love and not ego, competition, or wanting to rub your nose in your mistakes. We intuitively know the difference.

Below are some things to keep in mind when seeking support. People to surround yourself with:

- Others who have been in your shoes, achieved peace, and handled the situation well. These are comrades who have been where you are and have created stability. They're not still fighting with the other household. They've found a way to live in their situation, but not let it take over their life.
- People who realize your end goal is positivity and not to just continually complain. Surround yourself with those who support your higher-self goals and won't keep fueling the fire. These people will say, "I see you're really making an effort here. Even though it's tough and

there's still conflict, you're doing a great job."

- Friends who will let you voice your frustrations and then help you look for answers. They'll say, "Let's brainstorm some potential solutions. What are some other options here?" They understand the initial need to vent, but also know that the end goal is to resolve conflict, even if it's within yourself.
- Those who will be truthful with you. They'll see that your actions may be hurting you or your situation and they're not afraid to tell you so. These folks will say, "Actually, I think you might have been out of line there. What you did would have made me mad too," or "I hear you focusing all your anger on her, but I don't hear you taking any responsibility here."

She's the hero of her story too

Many problems between houses start because someone is just trying to solve a problem. A father desperately misses his kids. A stepmom is trying to feel a sense of belonging in a family with lots of history that came before her. A mom feels resentful including the stepmom in decisions that used to be between her and the kids' father.

People struggle with their emotions and act in less-than-helpful ways that don't "apply" to them. And yet it does—when they're in pain.

We excuse *our* actions because we know what's at stake for us. We forgive our own inappropriate behavior. We rationalize it because we understand our own secret motivations. But what about the other side? Where does your compassion for them begin and end? Can you see their pain? Is it possible to reinterpret their manipulative, crazy conduct?

When you find yourself on the receiving end of some extreme behavior that confounds you, it's worth considering whether you've touched a nerve that might represent some deep-seated, diagnosable issues. Sure, it can be petty and gratifying in the moment to internally accuse the other person of having a personality disorder. And... sometimes they do!

If that's the case, it's not your job to fix them. But, it might help you to know that personality disorders often have a core fear of abandonment driving their behaviors—even if those same actions almost seem to guarantee abandonment, sadly. Could your mere presence in the situation be triggering that fear in the other person? This is not to put the onus on you for dancing around their deepest emotional wounds. But with behavior that seems abusive and inexcusable, just understanding this possibility might help you pause and shift something inside of you.

Cultivate wisdom

Weeding out ineffectual support

Now that you have a better understanding of the difference between seeking validation and seeking solution-oriented help, take an inventory of which part of your support system belongs in which category.

- Which people stand out to you as steady sources of wise, helpful wisdom?
- Do you have people in your life who are draining your energy instead of helping to replenish it? People who feed the drama and negativity, instead of offering helpful advice?

Once you've pinpointed these roadblocks in your support system, think about removing them. Not out of your life, but out of your advice circle. For example, if Jane is great at jumping on the bandwagon and always agrees with your perspective, but isn't so great at brainstorming helpful actions, you know that when you're feeling like you just need some short-term validation, she's your go-to girl.

You may also have people in your support circle that don't fit into either category. Perhaps you have a friend who's better off being your gal when you need a new pair of shoes, but not objective, sound feedback, or validating your struggles. Maybe another friend is great to talk to about parenting challenges, such as a baby who's not sleeping through the night or playground battles, but not the stuff that's too close to your heart.

In the words of our readers

Aimee G. (stepmom): *"I have learned from my own stupidity that no matter how many high fives I got from my friends, it is not very wise to vent to all on Facebook."*

Holly O. (divorced mom): *"I have many people in my life all too willing to validate me when I rant about my child's stepmom. I had never lashed out at her, after many years of dealing with each other. Finally, the last time we argued (after being validated by a friend), I said those mean and hateful words you should never say to someone who has shared in the raising of your kids: 'Because I'm their mother!' I shouted it. It was hurtful, no matter how much she pushed me or asked for it. To me, I crossed the line. It's been over a year since we last spoke and I wish I could take it back."*

Renee S. (stepmom): *"I sought commiseration at first, which left me wallowing in anger and self-pity. Now I surround myself with wise women who ask me tough questions and keep me honest. It's improved not only my familial relationships, but my overall state of mind as well."*

Exercise: What kind of support do I need?

The next time you need some support, answer the following questions to regain your composure and pursue the right support path.

1. Scan your body

- Take a few deep breaths.

- How are you feeling right now? Which emotions are the strongest? (You may have several and they might be contradictory.)

- Where do you feel these feelings in your body?

- How would you rate your level of discomfort on a scale of 1-10, with 10 being almost unbearable?

2. Decide: discharge or connect?

- Do you feel the need to discharge some of that negativity first, before you'll be open to feedback from a friend? Or do you feel the need to connect with another living soul more?

- Discharge: If you need to discharge energy first, what are some harmless ways to do that?

- Connect: If you'd rather connect with a friend or family member:

    - Do you want a sympathetic audience who won't challenge your version of events?

    - Or do you feel a sense of open-ended curiosity? Are you willing to consider the possibilities of a different perspective?

- Verbalize exactly what you're looking for. "Right now, I just need some reassurance." Or, "I could use some help coming up with new ideas for what to do." Think about what you need to hear right now that would make you feel better. Can you also provide this reassurance for yourself somehow?

3. Wait It Out

- Rather than making something definitive and concrete happen, consider whether you need to leave yourself some space to come up with a great solution *later*, when you're in a more grounded state of mind.

Dealing with leftover resistance

If you still feel some resistance to seeking helpful support, you may have some negative beliefs operating in the background. Put a check mark next to any you can relate to:

- "My friends will be mad at me if I change too much."
- "If I stop venting to my friends, we'll have nothing to bond over."
- "If I seek out "truth-tellers," they may say something I can't handle."
- "I'm right and she's wrong and anyone who can't see that is crazy."
- "If I don't gossip, I'll seem too serious and boring."
- "I'm embarrassed about "taking the high road." I don't want to seem like a snob."
- "Now I have to follow the other person's wise advice or else I'm a coward or lazy."
- "It's better to just try to figure everything out by myself."
- "Honestly, you can't really trust anyone. Who knows what secret agenda they have?"

What are your thoughts about what you checked off?

Quieting the drama

There are two additional tactics you could try to get support during a crisis:

- Tell fewer people about a difficult experience.
- Stick to the facts with a shorter explanation about the event.

Tell fewer people

The more you tell your story to others, the more it gets ingrained in your brain. The more you think about it, the more it physically and emotionally affects you, and the more you keep sharing it with people. It's a nasty cycle that will keep you mired in drama.

The next time you're faced with a situation where you'd normally tell a bunch of people how you've been wronged, try doing this instead: share what happened and your feelings about it with only one person. Choose someone you would consider an "effective" support person and then see how long you can go without talking about it with anyone else.

Doing a deep dive, then setting the problem aside might help you feel less activated and affected. See if giving the experience less oxygen helps the fire die out quicker.

Stick to the facts

Just like it sounds, when you're sharing an incident, you only share the plain old facts. Leave out any opinions, feelings, insults, judgments, or assumptions.

If the opportunity comes up (for example, a friend asks you how things are going with the other woman or household) don't indulge in all the gory details. Use phrases like, "Same ol' same ol,'" or "Just the usual…" Below is an example of sharing the gossipy way and then using this alternative method:

> **The Usual Way**: "Oh, you won't believe what she did. She had the gall to email me and tell me that my child was home sick and vomiting and that she thought it was something *I* had given her to eat. Can you believe that crap? Who does she think she is? I couldn't believe she was blaming me! The nerve of some people. I told her I didn't need her giving me *her* opinion about my own child. When will that idiot ever learn?"

> **Just the Facts**: "My child's stepmom emailed me, letting me

know my daughter is home sick today. She thought it might
have been something I fed her last night. Annoying."

Can you see how one evokes all this emotion, and the other is
just, well, almost boring? This is a challenging exercise because
without all the commentary, it's more difficult to get your friends
on your side! But the first method sabotages you and your well-
being. The second keeps you present and responsible, out of the
emotional muck.

Now that you're armed with some new tools to surround
yourself with a more effective support circle, we hope you'll be
brave enough to consider additional facts and possibilities for
long-term challenges you've been struggling with.

The help you invite into your life can make the difference
between staying stuck and unhappy—or creating new insights
that blast you forward into healing and happiness. Which one
will you seek even if it involves discomfort? The advice that is
reflected back to you creates different possibilities, like alternate
paths stretching out into the future. Choose the one that sets you
up best for growth, learning and peace.

Jenna's story

One of the insights I've had about myself is that I seriously value
fairness. I get very triggered when I perceive something as unfair.
I feel like I have to make it right. I have to be in control of the
situation. Well, as we've said throughout this book, nothing in
stepfamilies is fair, so you can imagine how often I was triggered
when I became a stepmom. I just wanted things to be fair.

Thirteen years later, things are so much better for me. I don't
have to control everything, yet I still experience periods of
regression or getting triggered. But now I realize this is just the
nature of the beast. I can be feeling great for months, coping with
many stressors and then BAM!, something throws me off. That's

why support is so important. We need to surround ourselves with people who get it and who can hold the space for us when we're thrown off-kilter, and then help us stand up again. Being someone who's an introvert, a homebody, and picky about the company I keep, I was never going to have a large circle of support, but I was lucky to have just enough.

Jennifer's story

A little meta story for you… After getting divorced many moons ago, I'd deliberately steered way-y-y clear of dating men with children because of everything I'd learned about the challenges of blended families. And yet, dating a man with children ended up being the kind of shorthand language that led straight to my heart. He got my priorities, my heartache, and the ongoing problem-solving of being a parent.

But as an author in the blended family field, when it came to getting support with my stepfamily problems, I struggled. I felt reluctant to share the raw details with other stepmoms I knew through the book because I felt conflicted about violating anyone's privacy. I was overwhelmed and hopeless at times, hanging onto my marriage by a thread. I felt a new sense of respect for Carol, my kids' stepmom, and validated by her responses to some of my struggles.

It wasn't until I became friends with another writer in my neighborhood that things clicked. We could vent and share, listen and help each other process. Our rantings were temporary, in the service of trying to reach a better place and were absolutely confidential. We watched as problems ebbed and flowed in our households. Children grew up and left to live their own adult lives.

A friend who gets it is worth their weight in gold and can really save you. I hope you find not just one, but many.

Mantras for seeking support

- "Not everyone deserves to hear private details about my situation."
- "I can have friends and family I love and not go to them for support."
- "I will be discerning with the advice I receive from others."
- "Asking for help is a gift to both the giver and the receiver."
- "Sharing my honest experience gives others permission to be vulnerable as well."

7

DECIPHERING
MEN

For Dads, From a Dad / Balance / Contribution

For dads, from a dad

By Mario Korf

Dads, I know how difficult it is to crack this first paragraph. It's likely you're handling your shit and there's enough on your plate without having to read a chapter in some self-help book. I understand and I'll keep it short.

I'm going to make some generalizations based on a limited sample size, skewed by my personal perceptions. I guess this is my lame attempt at a disclaimer, and if what I describe doesn't suit you, then it doesn't.

Maybe you don't have a problem being in the middle between

two feisty broads, and you've figured out how to co-parent with your ex, and everyone is happy in your complex family unit. That's great, man, and I'm happy for you, but that's not my experience. I reckon this chapter speaks to the average divorced and remarried dad, and there are men on either side of that curve that I'm not reaching at all. So if you're the average dad and you're still with me, I'll share my story and hope that some of it resonates with you.

I'm not a therapist and I'm not trying to be your life coach. I've made mistakes and learned a thing or two from them. I might slip in the occasional word of advice, or a cautionary note, but I'm certainly not going to lay a bunch of "shoulds" on you or tell you what to do.

Horses and zombies

I was at the dinner table one day, briefing Jenna and my teenage boys about my plan for the Zombie Apocalypse. My scheme involved horses rather than a car, which we would ride to a large boat stocked with provisions (because zombies don't swim, right?) We all laughed and contributed to the ridiculous plan, and dinner went by with smiles. The next day, I got an irate phone call and emails from my ex saying that I must include her in these stories. She was livid I didn't rescue her as well. Never mind that I can't ride a horse, and that zombies don't exist. According to her, I had traumatized the kids by leaving their mother out of the story. Apparently, this was the equivalent to having her brains eaten by the dead.

I usually wad up this kind of behavior and throw it away, but it got me thinking. Did I traumatize the kids? Had I done something wrong? It took me a minute or two before I figured out the problem; she still thinks it's my duty to provide for and protect her. Somehow the ten-year span that included separation, divorce, dating, living with another woman, and then marrying her, became trivial details.

And that's women for you. I can't figure it out, but I understand that women see a bigger picture that encompasses all things, not just rational things. Some women more than others. If you've ever had a woman mad at you all day for something that happened to her in a dream, you know what I'm talking about.

Provide and protect

However you feel about it, women understand that it's a man's role to provide and protect. It's why rich old geezers and brainless thugs have arm candy that'll have you shaking your head in disbelief. And it's why you'll probably do or have done things for your ex that your wife feels like you shouldn't be doing. Maybe you extended an invitation to a family event, tried to include her in a birthday party for the kids, didn't charge her for something you paid for, or made some other kind of effort to help her out.

My ex and I did a lot of hurtful things to each other over the years, and my friends would be surprised to find that I still do the occasional supportive thing for her. She typically doesn't know about them, but I do it anyway. For example, I remind my sons to get her flowers on Valentine's Day; I don't nickel and dime her on the shared finances; I've rearranged my summer vacation plans around her (sometimes fickle) plans. Jenna asked me about this: how could I feel any charity toward someone who I've shared such a bitter and dysfunctional relationship with? Sometimes I wonder that myself, but I reckon it's because a man's instinct is to provide and protect, and this extends to everyone. Even the ones who hurt you.

Providing for and protecting your ex can send mixed signals. She might wonder "Why is he helping me?" After over-analyzing that for too long, who knows what she might come to believe about you. Or about you and her. So if you can make that decision to completely separate yourselves, maybe you're ahead of the game. I don't know, I can't help helping others, and I'm sure I've sent my share of confusing messages to, well, both women.

What isn't confusing is that I will provide and protect for my wife above all others. Part of that is never letting my ex speak badly about her. If my ex says something even remotely negative about Jenna, I immediately let her know that's not okay, and I will not be communicating with her if she continues. Setting a firm boundary with your ex reinforces that there isn't a you-and-her anymore. If you let your ex say something negative, she might get the idea that she's colluding with you. Sending the message that it's over and that there is no longer any "sacred bond" is important.

Just as I wouldn't let my ex say anything negative about my wife, neither would I let my kids disrespect her. Ever. If the kids disrespect her, they disrespect me. This is a message from me to the kids, not from her.

Fixing things

Men like to fix things, especially the easy and obvious problems in day-to-day life. A sticking door jamb or leaky faucet is our bread and butter, so when the women in our life start arguing, we tend to want to fix that as well.

And why not? Why should a simple misunderstanding between two grown women be any harder to fix than an item on a honey-do list? I don't know, but it's on the order of nuclear physics to untangle the web of a simple she-said-she-said between two women you married. Before making that mistake, realize that whatever perfectly logical middle ground you inhabit will be considered "taking her side" by both of them. My advice is to always take your wife's side, even if she's wrong (especially if she's wrong). It will not work the other way around.

Anyway, they'll figure it out, eventually. Or not. But it ain't your problem. The world would be a better place if we all just got along, but from my personal experience, it doesn't always work out that way.

Another thing that might not be worth fixing is anything in your ex-wife's house. Fixing a contraption that only you understand is a baited trap. A light bulb she can't reach is certainly easier, but may not be a good idea. Of course it depends on your relationship with your ex—these warnings are meaningless if everyone gets along, but if you have a high-conflict relationship, the list of things you can fix is short. I've learned to keep it all in my house.

When it comes to fixing things in a more general sense, your wife isn't going to understand some of the things you have to do. Oh man, this is going to get me in hot water, but there are things a man needs to do that his wife just doesn't need to be involved in. These are not bad things, mind you, or untrustworthy things, but details that she just won't understand. Women in general love to get all up in your business. They need to know the how, what, when, where, and why. But what they really mean by that is that they need to feel comforted, and that everything is going to be alright. But they mistakenly believe that knowing the details is directly related to their safety. Nope. Sometimes the opposite is closer to the truth.

You know what is best, and you certainly don't need my permission to do it. If this becomes the start of an argument, you have my sincere apology. Jenna and Jennifer will address this issue with your wife in another chapter, so don't press the issue just yet. Let's move onto the kids.

They aren't her kids

Your partner probably doesn't adore it when she's sitting on the couch and your kid's stinky feet are in her face. They aren't her flesh and blood, and she doesn't have the unconditional love for them that you have. But there's a certain strength in that, because your wife married you, not your children. She's there because of you, not the kids, or possibly in spite of the kids.

When she started dating you, it was probably apparent early on that she came second to the kids. Maybe more often than not. And you, charmer that you are, made her fall in love with you, anyway. Unless she made the mistake of dating other single dads, this might be the first relationship in which she experienced being second. That's a strange situation to be in, especially when the person is used to being number one, so it's important to keep her choice to be with you in perspective. I do this by saying the kids are my first responsibility, but my wife is my first priority. She is a wonderful person for marrying me (and dealing with my baggage), so I will put her first whenever I can.

Because your kids aren't her kids, she might feel resentful for the lack of reciprocity she gets from them. As a parent, we don't care if we give, give, and give some more to our kids and get seemingly nothing in return. We don't keep score. But day in and day out, she's cleaning their crap, making lunches, sending them out the door or picking them up at school. Or maybe she's doing less obvious things for the household, but equally important, like holding a job. What do your kids say to her for all this? How often does she get a "thank you?" How often does she get a "You're not my mom," or, "I hate you," instead?

If she feels resentful for giving all the time, that's normal. Normal people have a give-and-take relationship. Your wife needs to be reminded that her parents probably gave without reciprocity—kids behave like that. Certainly you can work on that with your kids: make sure they thank her or do things for her in return. That's part of growing up.

They are my kids

Whether your wife has kids of her own or not, she probably has her own ideas about how you're raising yours. This comes largely from how she was raised, but may also come from a need to feel protected in her own environment. She can't relax with the kids going wild, or the house is too noisy or too cluttered with their things all over the place. Listen to your wife about these things without getting defensive. She may talk about your kids and their less-than-perfect behavior, but she's not making value judgments about them. Don't take offense. Work to find a compromise.

Something I've noticed is that women in general feel that dads are too "hands off" with the kids. From an outside perspective, I certainly fall into that group. But it's by design! I lead by example. I don't micromanage and I give space for consequences to develop. Send a boy into the woods with nothing but a knife and he'll come out a man. Send him into the woods with everything but the kitchen sink and he comes out looking for mom. Men know this. Women, not so much.

Men who share that looser parenting style can be seen as not doing their job. Because of this, the stepmom may feel like she needs to "step in" and take on a more active parenting role. Apparently, this is a common phenomenon among stepmoms, because it often irks the moms and then everyone hears about it. The problem is that when stepmoms take on the parenting role, they do so without the one necessary requirement for the job: unconditional love. Unconditional love is why you don't need reciprocity, and it's why stinky feet in your face are cute.

But it's not that way for her, and lacking this essential requirement can get stepmoms in trouble with moms, dads, and kids. In addition, moms may feel like the new wife is taking over for the dad who is "slacking off," or maybe the mom doesn't agree with the new wife's parenting style. I can't really address how moms feel about stepmoms stepping into the parenting role, but I can address how I feel. They are my kids.

Taking on an active parenting role is one thing, and it can be a good thing if all parties are adjusted to that. But disciplining the kids or challenging your decisions in front of them is quite another. If she does that, you need to put a stop to that for a number of reasons:

1. They are your kids, and you know best. There's no arguing this point.
2. You probably disagreed with your ex on how to raise your kids, and you divorced her. The last thing you need is two women arguing with you about how you're raising your kids.
3. You want your kids to like your wife. It's your job to protect her relationship with the kids, and to make sure they like her. Don't let her make the mistake of becoming a disciplinarian.

Now, if your wife stays out of it, but privately tells you or advises you on how you're parenting, that's great. Keep it like that by telling her how much you appreciate her advice, and how it's so smart that she doesn't step in and sully her relationship with the kids. But if she's in the opposite camp, it might be difficult to relay this message to her. Maybe if she hears it from someone else (me), that'll help.

Stepmom: if you're guilty of disciplining your husband's kids or challenging his parenting in front of them, stop this now. Discipline isn't your job, even if he's not doing it (to your satisfaction). Whatever you think you'll accomplish isn't going to work well, and it does so at the expense of more valuable things. While the kids see you as an adult, and even as their dad's wife, you don't carry the same authority that dad and mom do, and whatever lesson you're trying to instill won't be nearly as effective as when it comes from them. If you're thinking of examples where your discipline worked, think about what you possibly lost in the relationship in return. Is it worth casting yourself in the role of the bad guy in order to get them to pick up their socks? Really, it isn't worth it. Please stop disciplining the kids and challenging your husband's authority. It creates a rift between you and the kids, and annoys the hell out of your husband.

What can you do? Discuss discipline with your husband and make sure it all comes from him. Don't nag him about it—that works about as well as a square wheel. If you absolutely have to do something about the dishes, the socks on the floor, or whatever it is that's getting your back up, try doing something loving and/or humorous. Eat in their room and leave the dishes on the bed. Put your clothes in their room before their friends come over. Do it with a laugh and it sends a better message.

Parallel parenting

Getting back to your ex, there comes a point where it's simply impossible to deal with each other's shit any longer. You probably both reached that point at least once already, and that's why it's over. But there are still the kids, and they need both of you. So you try again for their sake, and it works about as well as it did before. It might feel like that line from The Godfather 3: "Just when I thought I was out… they drag me back in."

After trying to make it work in a marriage, and then trying to co-parent outside of the marriage, I'm a strong proponent of parallel parenting. Here's a definition from the article, "Cooperative Parenting or Parallel Parenting?" by Philip M. Stahl, Ph.D.

> "In this style of parenting, both of you will each learn to parent your child effectively, doing the best job each of you can do during the time you are with your child. You will continue to disengage from the other parent so that conflicts are avoided. If you determine that you cannot cooperatively parent because your level of conflict is moderate or high, disengagement and parallel parenting is the necessary style of parenting."

Professionals often recommend parallel parenting in high-conflict situations. There's less to fight about, and less for the kids to be confused about. It works. I don't know your situation, so I'm not recommending parallel parenting to you. I just wish I hadn't made it a fallback option when things got bad. It's not a last resort; it's a parenting style that should be considered from the start, especially when parents typically don't agree.

So what if your ex doesn't want to do parallel parenting? Well, that's the beauty of it—she doesn't have to! Because communication is a two-way street, only one parent needs to make the decision. Once it becomes clear that's how you're parenting, she'll fall in step. There may be a volatile adjustment period, but that's how these things go.

If you decide on parallel parenting, a few things are very important:

- Don't badmouth her or her household. You are giving up the right to discuss the way she should be doing things, so let it go.
- Do not use the kids as messengers between households.
- Support the time the kids spend with her.
- Use an integrated communication system, such as Our Family Wizard to keep track of emails, expenses, calendar, etc.

I've done parallel parenting for a couple of years now and I can assure you the kids are better off for it. Not only that, but I'm happier, my wife is happier, and dammit, I think my ex is happier. Whatever fears you might have about parallel parenting are well founded, but in my experience, they didn't materialize. Children are resilient—they adapt to their surroundings and appreciate well-defined borders.

Rethinking zombies and horses

When I look back at that zombie story, I know I did nothing wrong, but I also know I didn't do it all right, either. If I could go back and tell the story over again, I would have included my ex, to say that she was safe or taken care of somehow. I still wouldn't have included her in my plan of horses and boats, because she's simply not part of my future. It's not rational or reasonable that I should have to do this, but it's the kind thing to do. And life's challenges (especially challenges with the ex) go easier when you're kind.

Thanks for listening, and don't tell anybody about my zombie plan. It's a secret.

The triangle of balance

Competing loyalties and obligations

So there you have it: one dad speaking directly to the other divorced and remarried dads out there (we were eager to eavesdrop too!) about his life as a remarried father. Many men seem like such unfathomable mysteries to women. We thank Mario for letting us in on how many dads experience the complex dynamics between two households.

Divorced dads are inhabiting three unique roles at the same time, like a comedian playing to three separate sections of an audience. Trying to make everyone laugh at the same time is tough-going. There's:

- His children
- His new partner
- His ex-partner

A remarried dad can easily feel like he's caught in the middle of an insane series of competing demands. But most men don't want to admit they're not up to any challenge, no matter how impossible. Thinking about what each party is expecting of him will help us understand why a remarried father feels pulled in so many directions.

After a marriage breaks up and a father remarries, everything changes with parenting and partnership. Mothers and fathers may have very different ideas about how communication should occur. How the hands-on details of daily life should be handled (and by whom). How the children should be nurtured and disciplined. How both parties should manage difficult emotions in order to successfully parent the children.

Adding a new parental figure into this mix often spells trouble. To simplify, we're going to focus on the combination of the two parents and the stepmother in this chapter and not the role of a stepfather.

In the words of our readers

Jenny P. (divorced mom/stepmom): *"Thinking deeper about how I was feeling, I actually was jealous! Not of my ex finding someone new, I was quite happy for him. I was jealous of my daughter's relationship with another mother figure."*

J.W. (stepmom): *"When I started dating my now husband, he always considered me a 'partner' and so my thoughts and feelings mattered to him. I don't think it affected his relationship with his ex at all, because she had no way of knowing I was an integral part of his opinion."*

Brynn (divorced mom/stepmom): *"We'd had a co-parenting relationship for 10 years that was working, then, all of a sudden, there was this other person in the picture. I had to just trust my ex-husband's choice and deal with it. It was hard, but I learned."*

Parenting and partnership

Disagreements over parenting and partnership are two of the most contentious issues between parents and between a remarried father and his wife. Two ongoing mysteries women struggle with when it comes to men's behavior are:

- How they show us they care (about us and others).
- How closely they're paying attention to the things we think matter.

We all have strong opinions about the best way to raise children that are frequently a carry-over (or a reaction to) the way we were raised ourselves. Our own emotional wounds and memories also inform our thoughts and feelings about the way we think things "should be done."

Let's take a closer look.

How men show love

Moms thinking they know how men should "be" with their kids starts early. From the moment a child is born, a mother often begins imagining how a child's relationship should unfold emotionally with their father. She may hover over him while he's changing a diaper to make sure he's doing it "right," make suggestions about how he holds and plays with the baby, and push him to be expressive with the kids in a way that she would be as a loving parent.

Stepmoms may form their own opinions about a father and his relationship with his kids when she and her partner begin dating. How close does he seem to be? How demonstrative? How affectionate? In the back of her mind, she may plot how to "fix" the relationships he has with his children, if she can imagine herself relating to them differently as a parent. It's all too easy for stepmoms to meddle if she thinks dad's not doing enough.

In Mario's story above, he talks about how he relates to his kids, choosing to be "hands-off" instead of micro-managing them, letting them learn from their mistakes. But many women, both moms and stepmoms alike, expect men to show that they love their children the same way they would: by asking questions, tending to needs and desires before they're even expressed, and by completing the endless, daily household tasks that signal to the people you love that you're paying attention. However, men may be focused on teaching their children more values-oriented life skills, such as self-discipline (how to accept authority and work hard), integrity (keeping your word and sticking to agreements), and honor (doing the right thing regardless of how you feel about it). This broader approach doesn't mean they love their children any less, though it might seem like it to us.

One of the best things you can do for your relationship is shift from wishing your partner would do things the way you would, to being able to see the gifts in their differences and then supporting and celebrating them.

How does your partner or ex give?

Place a check mark next to any of the behaviors you recognize in your ex or your husband below. Ways a man shows his love that you may not recognize:

- Teaching the child manual skills, such as how to build or fix something.
- Coaching an after-school activity or sport.
- Leading by example: keeping his word, helping others.
- Being attentive, i.e., asks about your day or the kid's day.
- Following up on discussions he's had with you before, especially things you or the kids are worried about.
- Being affectionate.
- Encouraging and/or helping the children provide holiday gifts for his ex or his wife.
- Going to work every day to earn a living and providing for your home.
- Paying child support on time or early.
- Fixing mechanical things around the house.
- Sharing technological knowledge with the kids.
- Helping with homework.

- Roughhousing with the kids on the floor or mussing up their hair, tickling, etc…

Journal questions: My partner's or ex's contributions

What did you learn about how your husband or the children's father expresses his love to you or the children?
Have you been overlooking any of these contributions and discounting them?

In the words of our readers

> **Kacey (divorced mom and stepmom)**: *"Over the past two years, my husband has surprised me with his patience and understanding regarding his high-conflict ex-wife. He looks at the situation, how his reaction might be taken and does his best to protect the children from any conflict between the two of them."*

> **Matty (stepmom)**: *"My stepson has always been kind and receptive overall, so that made it easier. His mom acted out, but my husband expected this and became more assertive with his own boundaries. I think it was good for my stepson and for our family unit."*

Recognize the contribution

Stepping up or slacking off

One of the major complaints we often hear from moms regarding their ex-husbands is that if he's remarried, and the stepmom plays an active parenting role, then he is being "let off the hook." Dad doesn't have to step up to the plate. He can fade into the background. It may be painful for divorced moms to see that men who divorce can indeed change, grow, and be better parents and partners—with someone else. Many stepmoms agree their husbands are 2.0 versions of their former selves and ultimately, that's a good thing for all parties involved.

There are three possible variations of what a father can become after divorce and remarriage:

1. He hasn't changed. He was disinterested and uninvolved before as a parent and partner and still is.
2. He has become a better partner, but still practices a more hands-off approach to parenting, compared to mom.
3. He has become a noticeably better partner and a better father.

It's easy to confuse numbers 2 and 3 above. This goes back to the differences between how men and women (especially mothers and fathers) may show their love. But as we discussed earlier, women will often step up to the plate without even being asked. The stepmoms in the second group who fulfill some of the parenting duties for their husbands out of love and partnership might be enabling some pretty unhealthy behavior—for the children's sake—and for themselves.

We mentioned competing loyalties and instincts in Chapter 2. Research shows that for the marriage between a father and stepmother to survive, it must take priority over all other relationships. This can be confusing as you wonder, Wait, how does that work? Doesn't that sound like neglecting the kids? Absolutely not.

As Mario stated earlier, the kids are his first responsibility, but his marriage is his first priority. The children's needs must continue to be met, but you must also negotiate some tough questions. Who's going to handle the enforcement of rules in the household after a father remarries? Who determines consequences for breaking those rules? Each "side" involved can have very different ideas about how discipline should be handled.

In the third scenario above, these fathers have remarried and, as in any healthy marriage, their partners have become integrated into their lives. Stepmoms will often do almost anything to make the life of their husband and his kids better or easier (granted, many times to her own detriment).

But here's the part that we think moms are missing when they confuse a dad who's not doing his part with one who's involved—he and his second wife are doing what happy, functional couples do by *practicing reciprocity*. And if there are now two adults in this household to raise and love the children, instead of one, why is that seen as dad escaping his responsibilities? This phrase makes it sound like he weaseled his way out of his parenting duties. There are some dads who are guilty of this. But there are plenty of them who aren't.

In the words of our readers

Tamara M. (stepmom): *"I think my husband realized the children wouldn't feel neglected or suffer just because he'd made a strong commitment to the 'new spouse.'"*

K.B. (divorced mom, stepmom): *"I assumed that once we were married, I would do more 'mom' type things for the stepkids. Nope. He wants to do it. At first, I was hurt and felt shut out. Once I talked to him about it, he explained he didn't want me to feel he was dumping his parenting responsibilities on me."*

Michelle (stepmom): *"One day when my stepson was complaining he was too tired to do his homework but had a big project due, I heard my husband say from the other room, 'That's what you get for waiting until the last minute. No more gaming before homework. ' I don't think it ever would have happened if I kept harping on him, making him feel bad about himself as a parent."*

Quiz: Making him wrong (for divorced moms only)

Place a check mark next to every sentence that you identify with over the other. Which statements can you relate to?

- ☐ "He should do everything himself as a dad or he's lazy."
- ☐ "It helps everyone if he has an involved partner, especially the kids."
- ☐ "If I don't get any help from a partner, then he shouldn't, either."
- ☐ "We all need help in life. I wish I could have my own wife!"
- ☐ "He's hurting the kids and he doesn't care."
- ☐ "He really does love them and they know it. But he has his own way and it's just as good as mine."
- ☐ "If he doesn't show the kids that he loves them like I do, he's damaging them irreparably."
- ☐ "I have to admit, they feel secure knowing that their dad would do anything for them."

Moms, what do you think about what you checked off above?

Is it possible that the second statement in each group is more true than you'd like to admit? Are you making assumptions about how your ex is slacking off, when he really just has his own style?

What can you appreciate about him as a father? How is he giving more to the kids than you realized?

Quiz: Making him wrong (for stepmoms only)

Place a check mark next to every sentence that you prefer over the other. Which statements can you relate to?

- ☐ "He's missing yet another opportunity to teach the children a life lesson about responsibility!"
- ☐ "He knows what he's doing and not everything has to be a lesson learned."
- ☐ "He's spoiling his kids by doing for them what they can do for themselves."
- ☐ "He's showing love for his kids by providing for them."

> ☐ "He shouldn't be so nice to his ex-wife."
> ☐ "He's a provider by nature and being nice to her helps keep conflict away from his family."
> ☐ "He's a pushover and lets the ex make all the decisions about the kids."
> ☐ "He's good at choosing his battles and sees benefit in allowing the ex to make decisions that aren't a big deal to him."

Stepmoms, what do you think about what you checked off above?

Is it possible that the second statement in each group is more true than you'd like to admit? Are there any areas where you're overlooking your husband's contributions? What aren't you giving him credit for?

Are there any areas where you can show him you trust him to do the right thing by taking a step back?

In the words of our readers

> **B. (stepmom)**: *"I let my husband know that it would be best if he refrained from saying, 'we think' in their conversations. Things are better now that he practices that with her and their correspondence seems to be less emotional and more 'business-like now.'"*

> **J.W. (stepmom)**: *"I feared I would always come second dating a man with kids and that I would always feel insecure. But my husband manages to be an amazing dad to all of his kids (now to include 'ours') and to always prioritize our relationship and our marriage."*

When he appeases his ex instead of his partner

Many stepmoms complain that their partner would rather make her angry than their ex. It feels like a betrayal. It leaves them feeling like this is just one more way they're at the bottom of the totem pole and their partner doesn't value their relationship or them. This breeds contempt for their partner as they feel unprotected and unvalued. But there are many plausible reasons for your partner's behavior, which involve a much less sinister explanation:

- If the ex-partner is difficult or unstable, your anger and hurt is easier to handle than the ex's.
- The ex holds the power of the children. Even if a dad has 50/50 custody, he knows that in many cases, courts still side with the mom. That fear of losing the kids is very real.

Most times, appeasing the ex is their way of protecting you and your household from the wrath of the ex—even though it doesn't feel that way to you.

Just because your partner may have good reasons for appeasing the ex at your expense, it doesn't mean it's a sustainable dynamic. In relationships, we need to feel that our partner has our back. We need to feel safe with them and trust that they have our best interest at heart. But when we see our partner giving their ex what she wants on a regular basis, instead of giving us what we want, we lose that trust. And it won't matter if our partner has good intentions. The lack of trust, and built-up resentment this dynamic can cause will wreak havoc on your relationship. We highly recommend you seek counseling as a couple if you're experiencing this. It's often too difficult of a situation to navigate on your own.

In the words of our readers

K.K. (divorced mom, stepmom): *"My second husband surprised me with his absolute refusal to blame me for my children's bad behaviour. My ex always made their behaviour my fault. I can't tell you my relief to know that he sees my children's behaviour as entirely separate from me."*

Matty (stepmom): *"My husband seems like the emotionally clueless nerd, kind of like Sheldon. But if I need to talk or something is up, he is a great listener and tries to get it."*

J.B. (divorced mom): *"I was really nervous when I was pregnant with our baby because my husband was never a man who thought he wanted kids. But he is a great dad, and that has made him an even better stepdad, way more well rounded."*

Coming into their own as dads

Men don't need us to micromanage their relationships as fathers. Just because they're not parenting as we women would prefer, doesn't mean they're doing a poor job. But many women are uncomfortable leaving any kind of vacuum for a father to step into. We see them hesitate and we step on their toes without giving them a chance to figure it out or learn something new.

It doesn't matter if you're a divorced mom or a stepmom. By keeping your nonessential judgments about his parenting to yourself, you give him space to learn and grow as a father. Lest that sound patronizing, what that looks like is up to him and may be the opposite of how you would do it. Some men just did what their first wives wanted them to do because it was easier than being criticized. Now that they're no longer married to their first wife, they've discovered that they can be the parent they want to be with their own choices and style. There may be some stumbling along the path, as with anything that you learn for the first time, but they'll find their way. Give them the chance to blossom as a father. Their children's lives will be all the richer for it.

Moms, are you setting your ex up to fail because you're still hurt and angry with him? How can you show respect and support for his path as a father? How might this help the kids?

Stepmoms, how can you let go of what you think is best for his kids and let him be the father he is? How can you better support his decisions, even if you don't fully agree with him?

Jenna's story

In all of my relationships, from my first boyfriend to my current husband, I expected my partner to behave the way I did. I expected them to show love the same way, to give me the same focus I gave them and to understand exactly how I was feeling.

Then I found Alison Armstrong and her research on men and women and that all changed. Things finally made sense to me. For example, I knew Mario loved me deeply, so why when I would speak to him sometimes would he just ignore me? I learned he wasn't ignoring me, he was just focused on something else and couldn't shift focus as easily as I could. So now instead of getting mad or hurt that I was "ignored," I'd just say "Let me know when you're done there, I have a question." Such a simple thing made a huge difference for us. I also learned so much about the differences between fathers and mothers/stepmothers in terms of parenting. I shouldn't expect Mario to parent the way I would. He's parenting as a father, and I'm not a father. And vice versa.

Studies around men and women can be controversial, and I don't have the expertise nor the bandwidth to debate that here. But what I can tell you is that studying the differences between men and women was relationship-changing for me, as well as hundreds of stepmoms I've worked with.

It's helped me understand Mario as a man and a father and why he would make some of the choices he made. I didn't always agree, but I understood. Now we're at the point where we just lovingly laugh at each other and our differences, call them out when we see them and appreciate each other for them. Which is so much more fun than fighting about them!

Jennifer's story

In many ways, the quality of our romantic relationship mirrors our relationship with ourselves, don't you think? When I was married to my ex-husband, we were like two little baby adults, trying to figure out all the grown-up things while we raised two babies ourselves. As we grew older, we grew apart instead of closer.

As I've mentioned here, meeting my husband and becoming a stepmom has invited me (so tempting to say forced!) to learn how to speak up for myself, implement better boundaries, but also, perhaps most importantly, learn to separate the difference between my own problems and someone else's. I'm a much happier person these days than I used to be, especially in my relationship. So many things that used to stress me out roll off my back in a way that still surprises even me.

But… as with all personal growth, sometimes, those are the life lessons that you go into kicking and screaming. The stuff that goes deep down in there, the stuff you usually can't see. That was what needed to change on a core level—and it did. But like all fundamental change, it ain't done yet. I've got miles to go… What helps me to know I'm on the right track is that I can look at my husband and realize: you are the person I still want to have problems with in my life. You are the person I still want by my side when we're slogging through the muck and everything seems hard and impossible.

Yes, sometimes my husband seems like the source of all those problems! But we always come back to a base of connection, of understanding and, simple though it sounds, of silly laughter.

If you can find that kind of relationship with someone, where even amongst the trouble, the sun still shines, do your best to protect it and take care of it. I'll continue to do that with mine…

Mantras for understanding men

- "I can create a healthy, balanced relationship."
- "Even though we're very different, our complementary skills blend well together."
- "I'm appreciated for being a strong, independent,

unique woman."
- "It feels good to support my children's relationship with their father."
- "We may have opposing parenting styles, but I choose to see his good intentions."

8

BUILDING YOUR SANCTUARY

Refuge / Renewal / Dreams

Create your refuge

The relief of being protected

We've spent almost the entire book talking about how draining these relationships can be between households. Now we're going to spend some time savoring that wonderful feeling of getting away from it all. A place where your needs are all that matter. Where you get to escape to the comfort of simple pleasures and rituals. A place in your home where you get to relax, enjoy yourself and feel cozy, warm and safe. There's the outside world, with all its problems... and then... there's your interior world with walls six feet thick, a fortress for you (and your family, but over there somewhere, for now). It's vital that you have a shelter like this. Because you're not just meeting life's regular problems, you're also managing additional conflicts between households at home.

This is your chance to prioritize excellent self-care. When you practice self-compassion and treat yourself with more kindness, your entire life can change. Over time, as you develop habits where you decompress, tune inward and recharge, you'll come to expect being treated with respect because you're already treating yourself that way. Anything else becomes easier to step around.

Most people unconsciously believe they have to wait until all their external problems are gone before they can take better care of themselves. Not true! Don't wait until circumstances outside your control are neatly wrapped up before you allow yourself little dips into the pool of contentment. Don't put your life on hold until you reach some vague, elusive state of perfection. You don't need anyone's permission to begin. Just prioritize yourself!

Look at what's waiting for you when you do.…

The happy side effects of prioritizing your needs

When we practice regular self-care, even small, positive actions can have a compounding effect in other areas of our life.

We can compartmentalize and set aside problems to protect our mental health. We separate someone else's pain from ours. We can determine what is our responsibility and what is theirs. We can detach with love. True, those lines get blurry when we see a loved one struggling and in pain, but it's easier to not take on the burdens that don't belong to us when we feel grounded and "ourselves."

We can directly ask for what we need, instead of silencing ourselves.

Instead of being afraid and trying to control a situation by manipulating people, our actions can come from love—for ourselves and others. We're not running from the possibility of rejection. We have the strength to ask for what we want without attachment to the outcome, using passive-aggressive behavior or hoping someone will rescue us. If it doesn't work, you don't get indignant. You simply accept it and think of a Plan B.

We can self-soothe.

We're able to make ourselves feel better instead of looking to outside sources. We take it upon ourselves to calm our emotions down and regain our stability. We see situations with more objectivity. When we know we have already done the work of tending to our upset feelings, we come to the other person with our cup mostly full, instead of mostly empty.

We can forgive our own mistakes.

Forgiveness makes room for change and forward progress. When you increase the well of compassion you have for yourself, it makes you a more mature, adaptable person. You surrender to the vagaries of life that can't be reduced to black-and-white problems, with one person in the wrong and one who's right.

To the extent that you can accept and even embrace your own contradictions and foibles, it's easier to accept the same in others and empathize with their ongoing struggles, even if it involves being on the receiving end of negative behavior. Forgiving ourselves is often last on our list of tasks when we're in conflict, but it's one of the most powerful ways to transform a difficult situation.

Quiz: What's your current sanctuary baseline?

How would you describe your self-care habits at the moment? Which of these thoughts below seem most familiar to you? Put a check mark next to the ones that characterize how you typically handle your own needs.

☐ "I'll relax later. It's more important for me to get everything done: attend Katie's game, take John to swim lessons, cook dinner, sort the laundry, get the kids ready for sleep, etc."

☐ "I have a million things to do, but my stress levels are climbing into the stratosphere, so I'm going to take ten minutes to catch my breath."

☐ "When I'm feeling overwhelmed or stressed, I usually think 'But how can I think of myself at a time like this? My partner works as hard as he can. What right do I have to complain?"

☐ "My partner is overworked and needs some relief, but so do I. I'll ask him for some time to discuss how we can better meet each other's needs—and our own."

☐ "I can't remember the last time I did something fun for myself, outside of the family."

☐ "Ooh, it's girl's night! I love my weekly get-together with friends where I forget all about life's stressors."

How'd you do? Do you consistently honor your own needs or put them on the back burner? If you're a back-burner kind of gal, don't worry. It's never too late to take better care of yourself, without the guilt.

In the words of our readers

A.W. (divorced mom, stepmom): *"I spend a lot of time on others' needs, to my detriment. I am very fortunate to have a husband who often sees my needs before I do and is happy to do a load or two of washing, or vacuum, just to ease the burden."*

Pat (stepmom): *"My 15-year-old stepson (whom I have known for 7 years) recently asked, 'Since when do you listen to country music?' to which I responded, 'Since I stopped caring about everyone's happiness more than my own.' That sums it up."*

Make yourself an "unreasonable" priority

So… enough of the toxic societal messages! Taking good care of yourself is not selfish. Women aren't supposed to be endlessly self-sacrificing. We aren't the emotional managers of the family, who have to help everyone heal and be settled and happy before we get to tend to ourselves. We deserve to feel good too, without having to "earn it" first.

Make excellent self-care a regular part of your life. Don't think of prioritizing yourself as something extraordinary, something that only happens once in a blue moon just before you're about to snap. Integrate these practices into your days and weeks, just like showering and brushing your teeth.

Yes, we understand that your workload as a single mom, a re-partnered mom, a stepmom, or a stepmom with kids of her own, equals a to-do list that's a mile high—and tomorrow it starts all over again. Still, we challenge you. First, imagine what a badass woman looks like: one who works hard and gets things done. But one who's also able to put her feet up when she needs a break and tells the world to go take care of itself while she gets some much-needed time and space for herself. Then, imagine showing everyone else in your family this same badass woman (you!)—and having them adapt to her—maybe with some grumbling at first, but ultimately, successfully.

If that idea still seems outside the realm of what's possible, think of it this way: if you have a stepdaughter or daughter, do you want her to grow up feeling like she always comes last? That her place in life is to be a long-suffering martyr whose efforts will be overlooked and taken for granted? Who will feel resentful and undervalued? If you have a son or stepson, do you want him to treat women that way?

Of course, the answer is a resounding no!

So let's talk about some tangible ways for you to make your own personal refuge.

Create a space you love that's all yours

It's difficult to focus on what you need if you don't have a comfortable, safe place that's your very own. Start thinking about where that place could be and what types of things you want in it. If you don't have a lot of space, it's time to get creative. We've seen women use a corner of a room or even part of their closet as their private refuge.

Once you have the space, it's time to adorn it with items that you want to surround yourself with. This could be anything from fuzzy pillows to oracle cards and incense, to a musical instrument and images of nature. Think about the things that bring you joy, that calm or energize you, that comfort you. It's in our feminine nature to want to have beautiful surroundings, so this is your opportunity to tap into that nest-building energy and create your refuge.

Here are some specific questions to help you brainstorm:

- What are some potential refuge spots in your house? Are there any unused spaces or corners that would make a cozy nook? Near a window? In a quieter, less used part of the house? If not, can you temporarily "claim" another spot as yours, such as a spot in the living room in the evenings?
- Where will you sit? If you're starting from scratch, add a cozy chair or even a stack of pillows. Make sure you also have a way to prop your feet up and that there's a flat surface nearby where you can set a drink, a book, notebook, phone or laptop.
- What else will be there with you? Add a blanket for winter. Perhaps include a stack of books you love, and pictures or art that makes you happy. Choose uplifting or grounding colors and luscious textures. See if there's an easy way to decrease the noise levels and increase the silence, like adding a privacy screen or curtains, or consider using noise-cancelling headphones or earplugs. Bring nature close with a window view or by adding houseplants. If you'd like, you can add collections of things that are touchstones of happy memories (a rock or shell collection from family trips, postcards, or letters from friends and family.)
- What can you borrow from other rooms?

See if there's any furniture, art, textiles, lamps, or end tables that aren't being used elsewhere. You may have to play Musical Chairs by switching items from room to room to make it work. Just think of it as a fun puzzle to figure out.

Prioritize renewal

Filling your cup

Now that you've chosen your space, it's time to think about how you're going to fill up your cup with the good stuff again, to restore your energy, confidence, and that feeling of just being grateful to be you.

What makes you wonderfully happy? What are the simple things you'd like to do in your private refuge—or elsewhere in your life? What are the basic pleasures you know you can return to again and again? Here are some of our favorites:

- Reading a great novel (ask your friends for recommendations).
- Listening to your favorite music, maybe even with headphones while you do something repetitive, like knitting or drawing or filling in a coloring book.
- Listening to an audiobook.
- Staring out the window, drinking a hot cup of tea or a cold beer, and just savoring some alone time.
- Brainstorming an interesting idea on paper or in a journal.
- Catching up with a close friend or reconnecting with an old friend on the phone or by video chat.
- Watching a movie or TV series that no one else in the family wants to watch, but you love.

What are some of your favorites?

Making meaning

What meaningful activities do you often assume you don't have time for, but that you know would bring you joy? Include supplies for hobbies or meaningful activities that you never seem to have the time for in your private sanctuary. You'd be surprised how easy it is to do those things if you decrease the friction involved in getting started. When everything you need is at your fingertips, you'll think, Hmmm, maybe I'll just try doing this for ten minutes and see how it goes... A collection of possibilities:

- An app with guided meditations or visualizations that you find relaxing and calming.
- A box with letter-writing supplies, such as beautiful stationery, envelopes, and stamps.
- A simple notebook or appealing journal, for a gratitude list, tracking Books To Read, or notes on books you've already read and enjoyed.
- Supplies for some kind of soothing crafting activity, like knitting, crocheting or sewing, even if you're "bad" at it.

A word about increasing the variety in your refuge: We have all become so used to being online that you may have forgotten the pleasures of being offline! Sometimes, even scrolling through beautiful images on Pinterests, posts from friends, or binge-watching a favorite show for hours on end can leave us feeling a little scrambled in the brain. Be sure to mix up your inputs and find a blend of both offline and online activities for the most balanced you. Sometimes, getting off the internet can be such a wonderful mental relief and a chance to rediscover that old feeling of endless mental and emotional space....

Trouble in paradise

So let's say you've set aside some Me Time, you're happy with your little corner of the house, but now that you're here, it's hard to relax and enjoy yourself. You may have some unresolved problems that are hard to set aside because they're important, but you don't know how to fix them. You may also have this sneaky feeling that you don't deserve to relax until you've handled things better!

When we don't feel good, it's tempting to just reject everything: our emotions, other people, the immediate future and especially ourselves. The antidote to this is radical self-acceptance. Make a conscious decision:

Resolve to accept all of you, just as you are right now, without changing anything.

Agree to be on your own side as a reliable, consistent ally, with your wonderfully flawed self. Worried, upset, and having a hard time or not. Say to yourself, "I accept myself exactly as I am, right now. That I'm stressed, hurt, angry, or feel like crying. I accept that I want something different right now. I accept that I don't have all the answers. Regardless, I still deserve to set all that stuff aside and RELAX!"

Whatever you're experiencing is part of being human. Show yourself kindness by accepting yourself in those moments. Then take a deep breath. Or several. Remember to make the out-breath longer than the in-breath, to activate the part of your nervous system that calms you.

You can also tune into your intuition and the wisdom of your body's inner pilot system to get some help grounding yourself. If you'd like, experiment by placing one hand over your heart and the other hand just above your belly button. Then ask your heart, "What wisdom or guidance do you have for me now?" "What do I need to know?" and see what pops up. You may hear a single word or a phrase. You might hear nothing at all or have something come to mind later.

Whatever the result, don't push for some miraculous cure to your concerns at the moment. Just give thanks for any feelings of increased equilibrium.

Then see if it's easier to do something fun for yourself.

When you consistently start making time for yourself to escape the pressures of life, you'll see some wonderful side effects, such as:

- The feeling you're living your life, not the life someone else wants you to live.
- A sense of competence and control over your destiny.
- Trust in your ability to make excellent choices and decisions.
- Compassion and forgiveness for yourself when you've failed in some way.
- Understanding for the mistakes of others.
- A good feeling about being open to others and risking your heart.
- Just the simple, solid feeling that you're really being you.

Keep reinforcing those good feelings with some new habits! Next thing you know it'll become second nature to take good care of yourself.

Small self-care practices outside your refuge

You may be tempted to just say, Okay, I've had a few evenings alone. Now I can go another three months, full-speed, without breaks, because things are about to get really busy! But that's what we're hoping to avoid: the personal deprivation that feels like running a marathon.

Instead, look around your day and see how you can build in little habits and routines that keep you feeling tuned in and tended. And no worries about making some big changes all at once. You'll practice your newfound tools off and on for years, adjusting and experimenting with what lifts your spirits and lights you up.

Below are some ways to implement this kinder, more nurturing approach.

- Bed yoga before you let your feet hit the ground, stretching and twisting just like a cat.
- Brief meditation, prayer, or expression of gratitude while you're getting dressed for the day. Think about three things in your life that you're grateful for and voice appreciation for them. (Your health, family, a roof over your head, a secure job, food in the cupboard, close friends, etc.) Name three every morning, no matter how simple. Repeating yourself is just fine.
- Setting a positive intention for the day, using an affirmation, or reading an inspiring quote. Keep an inspirational desk calendar by your bedside. Wake up, flip the page, and be inspired.
- Right after lunch, take a moment to check in with yourself. How are your emotions? What do you need?? Take some deep breaths and say a few happy mantras that make you feel good.
- Turn on some music and move your body for a few minutes to one of your favorite songs.
- Go for a hike out in nature, or just walk around your block. Try taking alternative paths and seeing what you notice.
- Take a moment before dinner or right after work to check in again. Do you need to take a couple of minutes to center yourself? Bathroom breaks are great for taking some "me" time!

Try this for 30 days and then evaluate the effects at the end. We predict that once you experience how this practice can positively impact you and your relationships, it will become an essential part of your daily routine.

In the words of our readers

> **Leila (stepmom)**: *"Walking in the woods with my dogs always helps."*

> **Kacey (mom, stepmom)**: *"In both roles, I would take some time for me (read a book, spa day, or do a craft that both the children and I enjoy doing together) and after each action of release, I was calmer and more able to evaluate the situation."*

Harness passionate dreams

Messy joy

This last section of the book is all about going bigger. Now that you're doing a better job of recuperating from whatever life throws at you, how can you reach higher for goals that are fun, challenging, and exciting?

We've found that the women who are handling the unique stresses between homes the best are women who are living full, messy lives, and would describe their lives as rich, varied, and ever-changing. They have enjoyable activities that they engage in regularly and pursue their passions. They have a circle of support, whether it's friends, family, or an online community, who accept them as they are, celebrate their authenticity and encourage them to be their best. They focus on adding to their lives outside of dual-family household problems and are so busy building a life they love, that their problems overshadow everything else.

So how do you become one of those women? Start adding more good things to your life. When you can't get rid of the negative (stress from the other woman), you can even things out by layering in the good, happy stuff. By enriching your life, the negative has less and less of an impact.

Here are a few places to start.

Try on a new (or old) identity

When you think of who you are, do you immediately think, "Oh, I'm just a mom" or "I'm just a stepmom"? If you feel that your identity has become a little lopsided, it's time to broaden your horizons. Now is as good a time as any to think about who else you are.

Think about how you used to characterize yourself before you had a family. Were you a rebel? An adventurer? Creative or artistic? A musician? Athlete? A bookworm? Out of all those different versions of you from throughout your life, which ones would you like to return to again? And what steps can you take to do so?

If you're one of many women who started in this role very young, or you feel complete with your previous life, then we suggest you think about what sorts of activities you always wished you could try, but assume you can't. You might surprise yourself! Think about people you know and even qualities in characters from tv, movies or in literature. What's calling to you?

Save the best for now

Are you still waiting for "someday" to come? We understand there are some things you just can't do right now, whether it's because of finances, scheduling, or other roadblocks. But there are plenty of things you can do, even if it means getting creative or putting a unique spin on it.

For example, maybe it's something as simple as having a private getaway with your partner. But you've been putting it off because it's hard to find a sitter for the kids, or because you feel guilty leaving them behind while you go off and have fun. Besides reaching out to friends and family to help you, maybe your getaway is a tent in the backyard, or a local weekend retreat, instead of the luxurious escape you imagined. It may sound silly or small, but these little things can add up to important memories and experiences for you and your partner. They are what adds to the richness of life.

So how can you do some creative problem-solving and still make some of your dreams happen? No need to save the best, most fun, most outlandish adventures for later. See if you can pull them off now.

See what you're capable of

Here's the problem with having dreams out there floating in the distance: there's no room to squeeze them in amongst the stuff you're already managing and the things you're behind on. So the answer to that dilemma is: you've got to drop something. But before you even get to that point, you've got to believe it's possible to take action on your dreams. Because it is!

Go big. If you had all the money, freedom and ability in the world, what would you be doing right now? Asking this question is a great starting point for thinking about where you might want your life to go. Is there a part of you that is yearning for bigger challenges, learning and growth, for stretching yourself and making a contribution?

Creating a vision board is a powerful way to discover what you're craving and how to make it a reality. The physical, mental and emotional energy spent creating the board and looking at it daily is a way to take abstract goals, explore them, play with them, and turn them into a concrete plan to manifest.

Take imperfect action toward your dreams. Just get out there and try something you've always wanted to do. Sure, we all have a variety of fears about not being up to the task. But screw fear! Just the act of trying can have an incredible impact on how we feel about ourselves. You might just find that you don't have to have innate talent to draw, sing, or play a certain sport, but with a little practice, anyone can do it!

Give yourself the gift of experiences and forget about trying to force an outcome that you can't control.

So, where have you been delaying making a move? What's something you've been wanting to try but have been too afraid or haven't made the time for? Go on. Call up a partner in crime, or if you're too mortified for your buddy to see you in a tutu, go it alone. But go!

Jenna's story

When something brings with it as much stress as being a stepmom does (or at least did in my specific situation), it ends up taking up most of the space in your life. It's what I thought about most often, it's what I talked about most often, it's where most of my physical energy went.

And then one day I just had enough of it. I realized the kids weren't changing who they were and the ex certainly wasn't changing her ways, so what else could I do to make things better for myself? Welp, I could shift my focus. Just because it was incredibly stressful didn't mean I had to add to that stress by being consumed by it.

So to start, Mario made me a spot in the house that was a kid-free zone. Not that they wanted to be all up in my business anyway, they were involved in their own things, but it was still a nice gesture. Then I made sure to have dinner with my friends and not talk about what crazy thing was happening that day. Instead I focused on them. What was happening in their lives? What fun plans could we make? I just generally made an effort to think about things that brought me joy, that added to my sense of well-being, instead of things that drained me. It made all the difference for me.

Jennifer's story

One of the women I have always looked up to the most is my maternal grandmother. She was wonderfully, deliciously herself, and did things that a lot of serious grownups wouldn't do, like ride the rollercoaster with me at Six Flags, sneak me dessert when I hadn't eaten all my dinner, or hang out with me in the kitchen in the middle of the night when I woke up from a nightmare. She seemed to live life on her own terms and was a beloved, vibrant character.

And yet… she lived a life of constant service. Cooking for every meal, ironing laundry, gardening, taking care of an enormous family, and making sure everyone was comfortable. Looking back, I wonder if she ever got one moment for herself in a week, much less every day. She died young of a heart attack, at only 63.

It wasn't until I was in my early 50s that I began to seriously consider the value of space and joy in one's life, as essential elements that were non-negotiable. It's so easy to fill up our days with to-do lists and fret about the near future. But we never know how long we truly have, cliche though it sounds.

So now, I'm determined to savor the smaller moments more, but also to see how I can create some bigger moments that are good too. You can cultivate a rhythm of appreciation and discovery in your life. Vow to stay curious. Let yourself still be surprised. The world is so big and random! What else is waiting for you out there, beyond all these divorced family problems?

We have a lot more power to shape our lives than we realize. And for that, we are lucky.

Mantras for Creating Sanctuary

- "I have the right to create a life I love."
- "I'm allowed to turn away from the drama and focus on what feels good."
- "It's okay to have ebbs and flows."
- "I can start living a richer life today."
- "I can still love my family and do more for myself."

9

ONE READER'S STORY

By Anita Inglis

When I first came into this stepmum gig, I thought I knew what I was getting into. I was a child of divorce. My step/parents had navigated that with a good amount of grace and cooperation. My parents negotiated their own divorce, my father would stay with my mother and stepfather occasionally, and sometimes with whichever new 'stepmother' was present at the time.

When it came time for my own separation and divorce, my ex and I disagreed on many things. But we agreed neither of us ever wanted our children to feel awkward about having both of us at an event. We had our moments, but mostly worked together well. When he introduced a new partner to our children, and they struggled with feelings of loyalty binds, I reassured them their dad was great at picking partners—after all, he picked me.

I told them I wanted them to be happy and to like her, and she definitely would want the same. The complaints largely stopped.

The recipe for stepfamily success seemed pretty simple. Put the children's needs first, behave like mature adults. How hard can that be! Way harder than I ever imagined, it would turn out.

When I met my now husband, he talked about his ex in terms that resonated with me and fuelled my hopes for a happy ever after for us all. He explained he would always love her for being the mother of his children, and would want to make sure she was okay because the kids were okay. Spoiler alert: one of the saddest things from our situation has been to watch that love turn to hatred and then indifference.

So I leapt into being a stepmum with my usual overachiever gusto. I had four children of my own, with whom I had made many, many mistakes. I would not make those mistakes twice. I wanted to impress my new in-laws by being Super Stepmum, especially compared to the children's mother.

But... it was bad with her. I won't go into details. However, things happened I had never imagined could ever happen to anyone, let alone me. I wanted to work with her, to create a safe, happy home for them, to support her as a single parent. I know how hard it is to be a single parent.

I just couldn't understand what she was doing, let alone why she was doing it. A constant refrain from me was, 'Why can't she see what she's doing to the children?' I went looking for answers, searching high and low to get some insight, and what I could do to make it better.

I stumbled across Jennifer and Jenna and their *No One's The Bitch* Facebook support group. It was like the answer to many prayers. It was a group of mothers and stepmothers invested in learning how the other half thinks and feels, and to learn and grow through those shared experiences. I'm not going to lie, it could be brutal. I had my a** handed to me many times, when my entitled stepmum opinions were out of line. I learned I am in the minority of women who are happy for another woman to take their kids bra shopping, teach them to cook, etc.

I tried all the techniques recommended by Jennifer's first book, and it didn't work. I concluded it was me, I was the problem. I began to hate myself for feeling so much hatred towards another woman. I struggled to know who I hated more—her for what she was doing, or me for failing my own self-imposed standards around how I should deal with someone actively trying to destroy my life and my family.

Eventually, I made myself ill with the loathing. Jenna came to the rescue. She had me recount the attacks I was dealing with, and asked me whether or not those things were hateful and worthy of my hatred. The answer was yes. What I was experiencing was really, really terrible. She gave me permission to feel the hatred and be accepting of that. It is something that has stuck with me since then. Those feelings of rage and impotence are something I have only ever experienced as a stepmom. In any other situation I can walk away and erase that person from my life.

Being a stepmom has been the most powerless experience of my adult life.

Within the group, it became clear I was not the only one living with this kind of situation and because of it, Jennifer and Jenna were inspired to write *Skirts at War*. Watching the book come together was such a relief. It helped me understand and accept that no amount of me changing or attempting to make myself acceptable was going to change my situation. It felt good to know I was not alone. This began my journey into understanding the psychology behind the way the ex behaved.

In the intervening years, I returned to study, gained a psychology degree and postgraduate qualifications, and trained as a stepmum coach with Jenna. Understanding the complex psychology behind the behaviour I once found incomprehensible has brought me peace.

I know the mom loves her children dearly. I understand she

has no idea of the pain and damage she has created for her children, and part of me prays that she never does because it would devastate her. After eight years of court battles, we've come to a 50/50 care arrangement, and this has enabled two of the three children to make up their own minds about much of what they have been told about us. The third has some significant developmental challenges and he may never be able to disentangle from the enmeshment.

We nearly lost all three children. If I hadn't had the support of both Jennifer and Jenna during the troubled years, and then supplemented that with my own learning, the outcome could have been very different. The underlying alienating behaviors haven't stopped. The outward attacks and false allegations seem to have. What has changed is that the children have had enough time with us to mitigate some of the misinformation and the years of teaching them critical thinking are starting to show results.

I'm now fortunate enough to work with other step/parents and families who are experiencing pathogenic parenting and alienation. Just yesterday, in a session with a formerly alienated adult child and her dad and stepmum, I could explain the pathology behind her mother's behaviour. I watched the lights turn on, and the tears flow. It was humbling to see that my experiences can now bring relief and clarity to other people.

I wanted to share my story to bring hope: there is a life outside of the conflict. We can create happy, strong family units despite the ex doing her level best to destroy them. The answer lies within changing our thinking, not her changing.

10

WRAPPING UP

Congratulations on reaching the end of the book! Looking at yourself with a magnifying glass is never easy, but we hope that you're on your way toward creating a permanent, positive shift within yourself.

Perhaps you realize that all is not as it appeared and that you have a much greater capacity to generate personal peace than you once thought. Maybe you discovered that you've been holding on to some resentments and judgments that can now be released. If nothing else, we hope you see that you are not alone and have many other fellow travelers with you on this journey.

We'd like to leave you with a few words from our readers. We've learned the most from them and hope their words will inspire you to shoot for the best in yourself, even though it might be hard.

> **Katie**: "I just wanted to say thank you for the last few years. You definitely turned my high-conflict situation into a success story. Three years ago, I never would've dreamed that the mom would become a regular babysitter for my children,

that we would sit with each other at ball games, or that she and my husband could get through a major custody schedule change without lawyers, mediation, and court rooms!"

Amber: "I don't have a friendship with either of the moms in my life and feel comfortable with that. I know I have done nothing wrong and we all have our own journey. I get along with one and have learned how to distance myself from the high-conflict one. It is good."

Aimee: "Thank you for changing my view on everything, especially my counterpart. Thank you for making our abnormal family and circumstances feel normal. Thank you for helping me grow, learn, and strive to be a better addition to our family."

Kelly K.: "Thank you for teaching me that just because it's the norm to hate your counterpart, it doesn't have to be that way. I spent a lovely day at the ball diamond with the mom, my future husband, my stepson, stepdaughter, my parents and my sister, and everyone got along. For the first time in five years, the mom wished him a Happy Father's Day."

Jeri M.: "I don't have the words to express what I have learned. Unreasonable hate removed from my heart. Knowing my feelings are okay. Peace in my home and peace in all my tumultuous relationships."

Lauren T.: "I've gained friends. I've gained perspectives I wouldn't get anywhere else. I've gained compassion. I've gained the ability to know it's okay to take care of me. I've gained more than I think I'm even aware of. It infiltrates into much more than just things with the mom, my stepson and my future husband. It's applicable to all aspects of my life and for that, I will forever be grateful."

Whether it's learning how to treat yourself more lovingly, how to not let that immediate fight-or-flight response determine your actions, or spending some time strengthening your boundaries, our aim has been to introduce you to some life-changing concepts to make your own.

Whatever you'd like to improve upon, cut yourself some slack, because personal growth is a marathon without a finish line. If all goes well, we'll all live to be little old ladies who are still refining our abilities to live happier, more loving lives right up to the very end!

If you haven't made as much progress as you'd like, take solace. Even the smallest change in your mindset will help you feel less stressed, anxious or angry and will have a domino effect on everything else. Your children and stepchildren's lives will be better for it. Your partnership will benefit. You are changing your family's future by modeling personal responsibility, forgiveness, kindness, love, and grace.

We wish all of you the very best and hope you'll stay in touch!

THANK YOU

This book is the result of first, two years of stops and starts—and then, eight years later, months of serious revisions during Covid Times when it seemed like the whole world was going crazy.

It's not easy to write a book with another person, especially when our two personal journeys have been so different. Luckily, we found we work exceptionally well together, brainstorming and filling in the gaps for each other's ideas. Plus, not many people can launch right into an old-lady sheep's voice at the drop of a hat on the phone. We make each other laugh so hard it's a little scary.

First and foremost, we'd like to thank the members of our NOTB (*No One's the Bitch*) community. So many of you shared your hearts and souls with us. Your stories helped us bring this material to life in a way we never could have done without you. We know your words will serve as a comfort to many new readers who are discovering these challenges for the first time. Many of you graciously gave us your permission to use your full name, but in the interests of protecting you from any future, unforeseen circumstances, we decided to only use initials for last names or eliminate them altogether. We hope you understand.

Several of our community members also served as early first readers. You worked with us on some crazily tight deadlines and your feedback and suggestions for improvement were invaluable. We owe an enormous debt of gratitude to: Laura Bonura, Jessie Marie Castonguay, Heather Coleman Voss, Beth Daniels

Olkowski, Gail DeVore, Mollie Ellis, Anita Inglis, Angi Kolthoff, Dina McCausley, Kathy Patrick Seligman, and Katie Price.

Jennifer would like to thank family and friends for their love, support and encouragement, especially my daughters, Madeleine and Sophie and my stepdaughters Kaili, Liza and Zariah. Warm thanks to David and Carol Marine, Annette Nixon, Erik Marshall, Rebecca Lincoln, Penny Van Horn, Crista Beck, Kai Woodfin, Karen Owens and Nathan Havlick. All my dear friends in my long-time writers groups: my brunch group, the Renegade Writers, and the Austin Writergrrls. And to the man who changed my life, Rhett, honey, a million hugs and kisses. You have my heart.

Jenna would like to thank: My friends for being there every step of the way. My stepsons, Zak and Mason, for putting up with me as I tried to figure this whole stepmom thing out. My husband, Mario Korf, whom without (for obvious reasons) this book never would have been written, but also for being my biggest supporter and best friend and for surprising me daily with your willingness and ability to grow as a person, father, and husband. There's no one I'd rather take this journey with. And most importantly, I'd like to thank my parents — all four of them — for modeling how divorced and remarried parents should behave. Thank you for raising me in a happy, healthy, conflict-free stepfamily. I'm forever grateful for that gift.

And last, but not least, grateful thanks to our bang-up self-publishing team: Karlem Sivira for fantastic and thorough editing, and Damon Za and Benjamin Carrancho for a book cover that gave us chills the first time we saw it and beautifully formatting the book (contact them at www.damonza.com).

A REQUEST

Thank you for buying and reading *Skirts at War: Beyond Divorced Mom/Stepmom Conflict*. We hope you found the book helpful and relevant to your biggest challenges!

As independent authors, we don't have a big marketing department or massive distribution in bookstores. If you enjoyed this book, would you please help us spread the word and tell a friend, share on social media or post a review on Amazon or Goodreads?

Thanks and much love,

Jenna and Jennifer

ABOUT THE AUTHORS

Jenna Korf is the owner of StepmomHelp.com and Stepmomz.com. She holds certifications as a stepfamily coach, feminine embodiment coach, and relationship coach. Jenna has been working with stepmoms since 2010, helping them to navigate their roles and overcome their stepfamily challenges. Jenna also offers a certification program training other stepparents, coaches and therapists in stepfamily dynamics. She's been featured on *CNN*, *Huffington Post*, *YourTango*, *PopSugar* and *Parenting*. Jenna lives in upstate New York with her husband and an adorable pup named Pepper. For more information about Jenna, visit her at StepmomHelp.com.

Jennifer Newcomb Marine is the co-author of *No One's the Bitch: A Ten-Step Plan for Mothers and Stepmothers* (GPP Life, 2009), which was co-written with artist Carol Marine, stepmom to her children. She's the mother of two daughters, a stepmom of three, a grandmother, and lives in Eugene, Oregon with her husband and two dogs. Jennifer's been featured on *The Dr. Phil Show*, *The Washington Post*, *The Globe and Mail*, *Publisher's Weekly*, *Library Journal*, *Psychology Today* and numerous radio shows and interviews. For her latest projects, visit JenniferNewcomb.com.

Mario Korf is a technical writer for Google and has published articles on motorcycling, spearfishing, and topics in between. His hobbies cannot easily be counted.

Anita Inglis is a mom and stepmom to seven children and the founder of the Institute of Step-Family Dynamics. She resides in New Zealand and loves to see her hard-won learnings empower stepfamilies and professionals working with stepfamilies globally.

Printed in Great Britain
by Amazon

82431339R00108